CHURCHMAN'S No.I CIGARETTE

.R.V.S.
LEVENSVERZ. MIJ
OPGERICHT 1838

Norwesco
PURE
ICE CREAM
SOLD
HERE

PICKFORDS
WAREHOUSING
HOUSEHOLD
REMOVALS
ESTIMATES FREE.

ÜBERSEE-TABAKE

Milkmaid BRAND Milk
LARGEST SALE IN THE WORLD.

ASK FOR
MARTIN'S
MINERAL
WATERS
HIGHEST QUALITY
FACTORY. EAST GRINSTEAD.

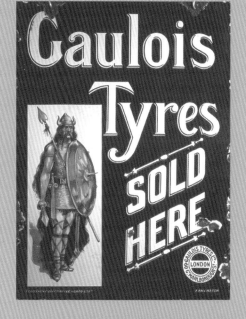

Gaulois
Tyres
SOLD
HERE

SPRATT'S
BUDGERIGAR MIXTURE
& CANARY MIXTURE

THE SPEEDY WASHER
"BALMORAL" CLEANSER SOAP
SOLE MAKERS OGSTON & TENNANT. LTD. ABERDEEN & GLASGOW.

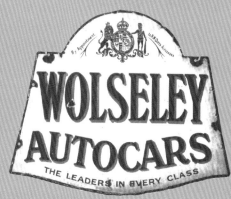

WOLSELEY
AUTOCARS
THE LEADERS IN EVERY CLASS

AGENT
FOR
W.&J. BOWIE
DYERS &
FRENCH
CLEANERS
GLASGOW

UNEQUALLED
WE SELL
"VICTORY"
-V-
GUMS
AND
LOZENGES
ALWAYS RELIABLE

NECTAR
TEA
1l PACKETS ONLY.

THIS IS W.B. ROBINSON'S PATENT
ERIMUS
DAMP PROOF PAINT
NORTH Rᴅ MIDDLESBROUGH.

Beam AVERY Scales
TIGER BRAND
AVERY
STOCKISTS

BOVRIL
BOVRIL WINE
Bovril Lozenges

GOODS RECEIVED
FOR
P.&P. CAMPBELL
THE
PERTH
DYE
WORKS

AGENT FOR
PULLARS'
DYE WORKS
PERTH
GOODS
Received Here

REMOVALS, STORING.
NEWBERY'S
FRIAR STREET, READING.

EDWARDS'
DESICCATED
SOUPS
BROWN. TOMATO. CRAVINA

AGENT FOR
BELLS'
DYEWORKS
PAISLEY

HIGNETT'S
SMOKING MIXTURE

THE ART OF STREET JEWELLERY

IF I WERE KING!

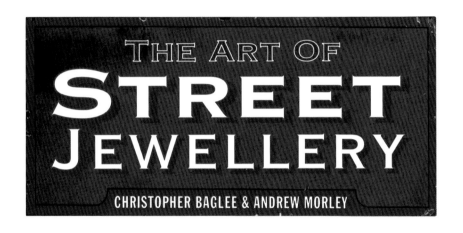

THE ART OF STREET JEWELLERY

CHRISTOPHER BAGLEE & ANDREW MORLEY

First published in the UK by
New Cavendish Books, October 2006

New Cavendish Books
3 Denbigh Road, London W11 2SJ
T: (44) 207 229 6765
T: (44) 207792 9984
F: (44) 207 792 0027
E: sales@newcavendishbooks.co.uk
W: www.newcavendishbooks.co.uk

ISBN: 1 872727 64 6

Design: Peter Cope with Andrew Morley
Editors: Peter Cope and Narisa Chakra

Printed and bound in Thailand by
Bangkok Printing Co., Ltd.

Enamel plate produced by
A. J. Wells & Sons Ltd.
www.ajwells.co.uk

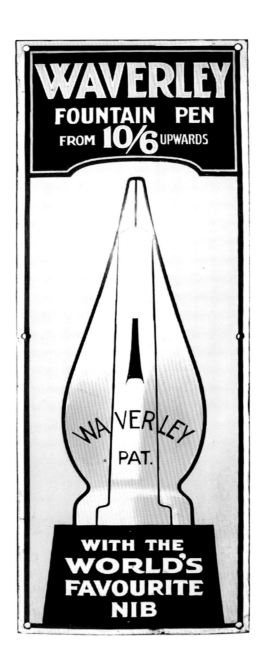

Contents

Acknowledgements

In 1982, our second book on enamel signs *More Street Jewellery* ended with a suggestion that an enthusiasts' club be formed. In the intervening quarter century the Street Jewellery Society's 350 past and present members' support and encouragement has underpinned our efforts in producing over 70 newsletters and reviews for the membership, plus two further books on street jewellery. Their contributions – of photographs, archival material, oral histories and general expertise – have enabled us to prepare this, our largest work on the subject. To them we are most grateful.

Many other individuals and organisations, particularly our fellow authors from other countries, have also been of huge assistance. Their names and those of others who have been of particular help are listed below. We would like to offer particular thanks to a handful of people (indicated by asterisk) who have recently thrown open their homes and collections for us and photographers Simon Danby and Alan Hayward to take photographs for this volume.

The enormous help given to us by many people since 1976 in preparing our previous three Street Jewellery books was, of course, acknowledged in those volumes. However, we are delighted to reiterate our sincere thanks to them along with new contributors. We hope that everyone involved has been credited by name or by organisation. If we have omitted anyone, please accept our apologies.

Alfred Dunhill Ltd, *Beamish Museum, Birmingham City Library, Dulwich Picture Gallery, Eton College, English Heritage National Monuments Record, Escol, Gateshead Library, London Borough of Brent Archive, M&GN Circle, Sheffield Railwayana Auctions, The Master and Fellows of St John's College Cambridge, Tyne & Wear Museums, The National Trust: Wallington, Wolverhampton Library, Museum für Gestaltung Zurich, Maidstone Museum.

Rosemary Allen, Mikhail Anikst & Elena Chernevich, Vikram Bachhawat, Mario Baeck, Mave Baglee, Roy Baglee, *Marcus Barber, John Barnicoat, Gil Bennet, F Bertin, Alan Blakeman, John Boyd & Sue Townsin, Elsecar Heritage Centre, *Fred Brumby, Mike Bruner, *Steve Burton & Eileen Burn, Erhard & Evamaria Ciolina, Birgitta Conradson, P Courault, Frédérique Crestin-Billet, Simon Danby, *Eddie Dunne, U. Feuerhorst, *Kath & Stu Furness, John Gall, John Juhler Hansen, *Johnny Harris, Jonathan Harrison (St John's College Cambs), *Colin Harvey, Mary Hayward, Alan Hayward, Diana & Geoffrey Hindley, Laszlo Ivanyi, Stefan & Sharon Jakobek, David Jones, Wade Kidwell, Guido Krummenache, Bob Lucas, Sue & John Markall, Andreas Maurer, *Bill McAlpine, John McGrellis, Olle Nessle, *Nicholas Oddy, Ian Parmiter, Moira Prusch, Jan de Plus, Klaus Pressman, *Richard & Judi Quinton, Howard Raine, Jurgen Renke, Alex Riepenhausen, *Stuart Searle, Frank Sharman, Jeff Sherrill, Caroline Simpson, Michael Snodin, J Stakenborg, *Mike Standen, H. Steinle, John Styles, Peter & Pauline Thornton, Peter Tydeman, Tony Verity, Bart de Visser, Micky Waue, David West, Michel Wlassikoff, Christopher Wood, Sylke Wunderlich, Susanne & Alexandre Zacke, J van Zadelhoff.

The authors

Andrew Morley, left and Christopher Baglee, right, photographed with their collections in 1980 and at Beamish Museum in 2000.

The authors met when they were students at Newcastle University, from which Andrew graduated in Fine Art and Christopher in Architecture. Having collected enamel signs since the mid 1960s, Christopher and Andrew joined forces in 1975 to organise their touring exhibition *100 Years of Enamel Signs*, which toured the UK from 1978 to 1980. They have been the leading authorities on enamel advertising signs since their first book, *Street Jewellery* was published in 1978.

In 1983 they formed the *Street Jewellery Society*, an organisation devoted to promoting, collecting, conserving and the appreciation of the heritage issues pertaining to enamel signs.
The Society has members from all over the world and publishes a magazine twice a year.

The Art of Street Jewellery is the fourth in the *Street Jewellery* series of books, bringing together images of enamel signs from around thirty countries.

The authors may be contacted and prospective members for the *Street Jewellery Society* may make contact at the following websites:
www.streetjewellery.com   www.streetjewellery.co.uk   www.streetjewellery.org

Dedication

This book is dedicated to the past and present members of the *Street Jewellery Society*
and to our fellow authors on this subject

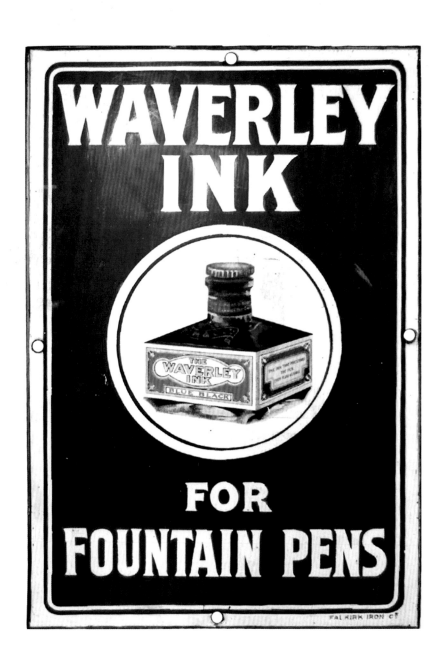

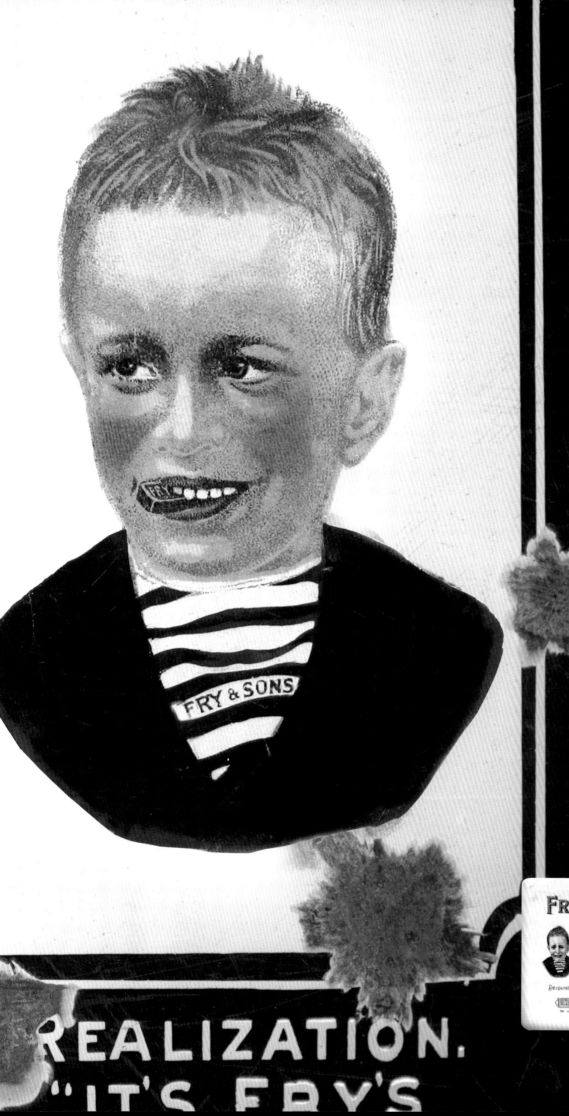

REALIZATION. "IT'S FRY'S

The Fry's Five Boys logo is one of the most enduring and well-recognised advertising images ever. It was issued in 1886 to promote all Fry's cocoa and chocolate brands, becoming a classic design icon when, in 1902, it was used on the wrapper of the milk chocolate bar. The Five Boys are in reality one boy, photographed in five moods ranging from 'desperation', quietening to 'pacification' as he is soothed by the offer of chocolate. The Five Boys famously feature on a series of enamel signs, including several colour lithograph versions. The fifth face, 'Realisation, It's Fry's', is shown on this page.

Foreword

by the Hon. Sir William McAlpine, Bt

My interest in enamel advertising signs started many years ago and they continue to excite my imagination. My collection of them forms an adjunct to the collection of railway bygones at my museum at Fawley.

Family and business contacts with the north-east of England led in the 1980s to my becoming acquainted with the authors of *Street Jewellery*, with whom I exchanged views and opinions on the subject of collecting enamels. Later I joined the Street Jewellery Society, a club for collectors of enamel signs, eventually being asked to become its patron. It is in this context that I am pleased to present the foreword to Baglee and Morley's latest book on street jewellery.

I am no stranger to sharing my enthusiasm for enamel signs, as I give fellow enthusiasts an opportunity to meet together and discuss, admire and swap railway and advertising collectables every couple of years, when I and the volunteers at Fawley invite other enthusiasts to an Open Day. On these occasions collectors have often asked the *Street Jewellery* authors when their next book on enamels will appear. Their reply has usually boiled down to 'as soon as we have enough material', followed up by requests for pictures of 'new' signs to include in such a publication. I am pleased to say that very many of those asked have generously provided photographs of their prize items in order that the authors might have new material to publish. Photographer Alan Hayward came to photograph some of the signs in my collection for the same purpose, so I will be examining this volume with 'half an eye' on which ones illustrated herein are from my museum!

The authors have suggested that I might 'open' the book with a look at what, to most collectors, and many others is the most famous enamel sign, the so-called Fry's Five Boys and the associated set of enamels by the acclaimed Edwardian illustrator Tom Browne. This will be the first time that images of all these versions have been published together. The Five Boys is an advertisement that I remember from my youth when it adorned the platforms and waiting rooms of railway stations, shop counter fronts, and the walls of countless corner shops. The face of the boy who posed for the original photographs in the late 1800s turns from tears to laughter as he is mollified by the offer of Fry's chocolate. It is said that in order to induce the tears for his act of 'desperation' and 'pacification', he was required to take a sniff of ammonia! Careful observation of the ruffled hair in 'expectation' might suggest that after this unpleasantness someone patted the lad's head to encourage recovery! Whatever the truth of the matter, legends of this sort have grown up around many vintage adverts, and lend further charm to them.

I am sure that if you have examples of enamel signs that don't appear in the *Street Jewellery* books, or have interesting anecdotes about such adverts, the authors, whose researches will continue even after the publication of this book, would be pleased to hear from you.

For now I hope that with the publication of this book, public awareness may be heightened and even greater appreciation of the subject be may be encouraged.

Photographic imagery had been rare in advertisements up to the time of the design of the Five Boys logo and remained unusual for decades to come. The monochrome images on the wrapper and mid to large size chocolate signs (page 1) are clearly photographic. The coloured versions, as shown here, are artists' impressions of the photographs, executed as hand-drawn lithographs, as colour photography was not yet commercially viable. Shown above is one of the faces, 'Acclamation', from a later production.

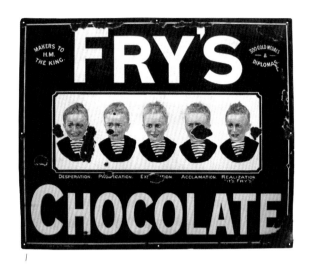

1

2

3

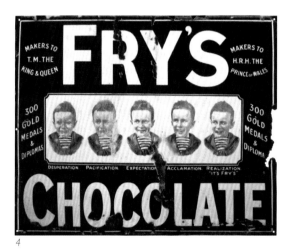

4

5

6

7

8

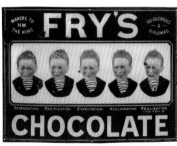

9

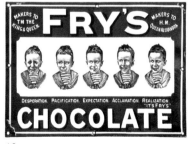

10

During its long pre-eminence as an advertising icon, the Five Boys enamel sign went through many permutations, including the earliest (5) which has no reference to royal patronage, but is assumed to be the earliest, issued near to the end of Victoria's and the start of Edward VII's reigns. Most Edwardian and later versions have dark blue backgrounds, but there is one with a green background, apparently dedicated to the Irish market (10) and there is said to be a red background version.

Technology for commercial reproduction of photographs was available by the late 1890s. However, the use of photography in creating this image was still unusual and innovative for the early 1900s. The faces on the Edwardian small (5/6), medium (9), uniquely with a yellow line round the border, and large format (1) signs, plus the George V coloured version (3), are drawn lithographs, based on photographic prints. All the sepia and black and white versions of the reign of George V (2/4/7/8/9) are actual photographs reproduced through decalcomania, printed in photographic half-tone, the leading-edge print technology of the time. On page 1 is a detail from the earliest type, reproduced near life-size, to show the granular, 'dot' effect typical of lithography. There is a clear difference between the faces reproduced by lithography (litho drawings based on photographs), and by direct photographs, whether reproduced by photolitho or photogravure.

Not all the damage to the above signs resulted from depredations by small boys with catapults! Many signs, once dismounted from their original sites, were re-cycled by allotment holders, so some of the damage holes were made by gardeners nailing signs to fences or cobbling them together to make sheds. The damage to sign 7 results from decades of slow erosion in a rubbish pit, from whence it was excavated by bottle diggers.

The three groups shown here are not reproduced to scale. The face panels on the large and medium format signs are identical in size. The actual widths are: (1-4, 10) 915mm, (5-7) 760mm, (8 & 9) 455mm.

1

2

3

4

5

6

7

8

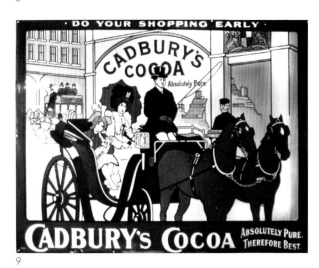

9

10

11

12

13

Tom Browne created a famous series of cartoons for Fry's chocolate, based on two well-known quotations: 'One touch of nature makes the whole world kin', from Shakespeare's Troilus and Cressida and 'So near and yet So far', from Tennyson's In Memoriam. All the cartoons were issued as advertising postcards, while two of them were also issued as enamel signs. On these pages all the postcards plus all known versions of the enamels are shown. In several of the images, the small white-background version of the Five Boys enamel (or a card version of it as seen on page 156) appears hanging in the shop window. In 'So near and yet So far', what must represent an enamel sign is displayed below the window. It is possible that the models for this are the two blue and white lettered signs (1/2), which may have been conflated in Browne's imagination to become the sign in the cartoon. Enamel signs were sufficiently flexible to be fixed in a shallow curve such as that of a bow window.

Browne also entertains us with two sly jokes hidden in the titles of the bundle of books which includes a book in the pile with the title 'A Few Facts About Cocoa!' Alongside rich pictorial imagery, Browne supplies plenty of in-jokes and verbal puns much appreciated by the Edwardians. The boy's strapped-up books might even allude to Huntley & Palmer's Christmas biscuit tins (issued at about the same time) in that form.

Browne makes visual reference to two images that would have been familiar to an Edwardian audience. One is TP Hall's sentimental painting 'One Touch of Nature Makes the Whole World Kin' (7), which was well known through exposure in mass reproduction, having been an instant hit when exhibited in about 1868 at the newly established 'people's' south London Art Gallery. The other is the image of a 'little rich girl' being conveyed in a landau, made famous by Fry's great rivals Cadbury in their 1902 enamel sign 'Do Your Shopping Early' (9), lampooned in Browne's postcard version (13). The 18th century-style bow-fronted shop depicted throughout and on the South Shields shop (8), was already 'olde worlde' at the turn of the 19th century. Later advertisers were clearly aware of the impact of Browne's imagery, as evidenced by the 1930s group shot of schoolboys and street urchins regimented together by the top-hatted Eton schoolboy type on page 6, (6). Characters like these, Lord Snooty and his Pals, were brought to life in 1938 by Dudley D Watkins, in his much-loved comic strip for the Beano.

These examples are among the first advertisements within advertisements.

Other forms of advertising which appear in Browne's cartoons were commonplace on shop windows up and down the country. Individual enamelled copper letters spelling FRY'S CHOCOLATE were glued to window panes (3). These enamelled copper letters like the 'F' (2) were manufactured in their millions by Garnier and other enamellers, to be attached with mastic to shop windows.

1

2

3

The evidence from photograph (4) suggests that signs were placed randomly to fill available space. The Fry's Five Boys sign seems to have been a late arrival, having been relegated to a garden wall adjacent to the shop. The enamel signs in this photograph have been accentuated by light colour tinting to distinguish them from other signage.

4

5

6

FRYS PURE CONCENTRATED COCOA

FRYS CHOCOLATE

TRY BLACK~GREENS TEA

COLMAN'S D.S.F MUSTARD

COLMAN'S STARCH

COLMAN'S STARCH

COLMAN'S D.S.F MUSTARD

HUDSON'S DRY SOAP

HUDSON

HUDSON'S DRY SOAP

KEEN'S D.S.F.

KEEN'S D.S.F.

NESTLES MILK

NESTLES MILK

LYONS TEA

LYONS TEA

BORWICK'S BAKING POWDER

BORWICK'S BAKING POWDER

HUDSONS

HUDSONS

HUDSONS

LYONS TEA

LYONS TEA

BORWICKS BAKING POWDER

BORWICKS BAKING POWDER

BORWICKS BAKING POWDER

£1000

£1000

VIRGINIA

CORAL FLAKE

CORAL FLAKE

7

William Bell Scott

In the 19th century, the Northumbrians Show the World What Can be Done with Iron and Coal.
1860, Wallington Hall, Northumberland.
Courtesy The National Trust, Wallington.

With this great paean to 19th-century industrialisation Bell Scott created an icon for the Steam Age. While the image swarms with references to 'Technology', there are only side glances at 'Commerce'. It was up to Benjamin Baugh contemporaneously running Salt's Patent Enamel Company in Birmingham, taking out patents for enamelling iron and exhibiting in the 1860 London Exhibition, to create the enamel sign, the metal medium that carried the hard commercial message.

Preface

The emergence of modern advertising art.
From Victorian street advertising to the 21st century art gallery

At the start of the 19th century, the marketing means and methods available to manufacturers and all those wishing to sell products and services had hardly evolved since trade began. The situation changed rapidly in Britain from around 1800, as the emerging Agrarian/Industrial Revolution overturned age-old working processes and conditions. Traditional British agriculture and manufacture, that had taken hundreds of years to evolve, were superseded within a few decades.

During the Industrial Revolution, changes began to affect all aspects of the daily life for the working population, beginning with a rapid incursion of newly invented or machine modified traditional manufacturing techniques and processes. As the Revolution took hold, the whole spectrum of activities associated with industry including commerce, changed. Part of this change was that two commercial factors – specialist shops and specialist advertising – evolved and spread rapidly. The phenomenon was recognised by Napoleon, who famously derogated the English as being a 'nation of shopkeepers'.

A new emphasis, on product, gripped the market. Many foods and items of use that had traditionally been home-made or locally produced or sold in an unprocessed state at open markets, were replaced by manufactured branded goods sold in permanent, dedicated establishments – shops. The novelty of branded goods, and the rivalry between manufacturers, created a need for marketing devices that would appeal to the public. Accordingly, advertising – 'the handmaiden of commerce', became more alluring. Enamel signs became an integral part of this process.

The social tumult caused by the Industrial Revolution and the Napoleonic wars shook off more than traditional working ways. Ever since the social upheavals of the Commonwealth, great changes in religious and political practices gave a greater political voice to the mass of the British population. In tracts, sermons and speeches, representatives of radical religion and politics inveighed against the social consequences of the Industrial Revolution. Fundamentalists found many commercial innovations morally repugnant. Universal Bible learning lent popular opinion a simplistic, fervour, which when directed against industry, quickly identified convenient scapegoats, including what were perceived as mendacious marketing techniques. So early in life, modern advertising gained a soiled reputation. Then as now, bigots regarded advertising as a hooker of the public purse and reviled it in Biblical language. Victorian morally upright commentators across the religious spectrum condemned the outward trickery of commerce (including advertising) as a latter day 'Whore of Babylon'. Self-appointed pundits, claiming to represent public opinion, have not ceased in the intervening years from condemning advertising and its associated art as unworthy of serious consideration.

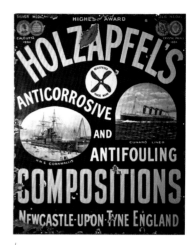

1

Bell Scott's Newcastle quayside (page 8) bustles with tall ships that were soon to be ousted by ironclads with smoking funnels. Holtzapfels (1) was just one of many Tyneside companies that catered to the ship-building industry. The value of having enamelled iron signs to advertise to such a narrow target market may seem strange, but product placement was recognised as good marketing practice even then, and was a tactic used by other makers of anti-fouling compositions, Suter Hartmann and Jahtjen's & Porters.

Napoleon's remark about Britain and shop-keepers seems to be confirmed by these enamel signs which portray department stores. The Midland Drapery building in Derby was demolished in 1970. Images (2) and (3) are details of signs reproduced in full on pages 168/169. Image (4) is an enlarged detail of (2).

2

3

4

However, criticism of this sort has not driven advertising art away. On the contrary this ostracism had and continues to have a freeing effect on the nascent art form. Excised from the respectable canon, commercial art was able, like other marginalized cultural phenomena, to develop without restraint. Freed from the bonds of decorum and convention, it has been able to interpret vividly social reality for each generation. Holding up a merciless mirror to society, advertising art reflected daily life with a frank liberality denied to the more formal fine art. In his foreword for the first British poster exhibition catalogue (1894), J Thacher Clark wrote, '...*in no other branch of design do the most characteristic features of every-day life find clearer expression than in the art of the pictorial and mural advertisement*'.

For over a century, an intellectual chasm divided 'commercial art' and 'fine art' in the minds of Establishment pundits. With the dawn of the 21st century, this dismissiveness shows some evidence of softening. At the start of this century, demonstrations on the steps of Tate Britain (aimed at eliciting public support for advertising art to be enshrined in 'serious' art galleries), could in the long-term result in success. In future, visual arts museums may devote sections to (both still and moving) advertising images. Indeed there may eventually be no 'class' distinction drawn between fine and commercial art. This blurring of the fine art / commercial art definition was set in motion by artists themselves, even before the Pop Art movement of the 1960s. Old Master painters including Leonardo da Vinci, Caravaggio, Rubens and Watteau were occasionally commissioned to create artworks to promote products, services, guilds, political parties and so on. Several French fine artists of the late 19th century notably Manet and Lautrec, enjoyed brief forays into the poster medium. The defining moment occurred in the 1890s, signalling a complete crossover from fine art to commercial art, when *Bubbles* by Sir John Millais was purchased by Pears and modified to advertise their soap.

That *Bubbles* became so widely familiar to the 19th century British population, is an indicator of the new popularity of Art, further attested to by numerous other cheap engravings and lithographs copied from famous paintings, known to have decorated the homes of all classes of society. Social historians appreciate the significance of such prints and have included the phenomenon in their understanding and interpretation of the culture of working-class home environments. Ordinary people indulged their new appreciation for art by hanging framed prints, illuminated religious tracts and three dimensional icons, and decorating their

BUBBLES,
by Sir John Millais B.ᵗ PRA

homes with ceramics and fabrics. Popular art such as that found in the home, was not the only 'refined' pictorial imagery to be appreciated as 'everyday' art. What is seldom recognised by social historians is that between the 1880s and 1930s, a form of advertising defined by the nature of the medium in which it was made, namely enamelled iron, surfaced as the 'Art of the People'.

The working population had immediate access to these permanently exhibited artworks, just outside their front doors. The 'poor man's picture gallery', as a quipping Victorian dubbed outdoor advertising, was probably a reference only to (temporarily pasted up) lithographed

paper posters. However, the dominance of these ephemeral posters waned when, from the 1880s, two generations grew up with virtual art galleries of enamel signs permanently fixed to the outside walls of their own and their neighbours' shops and houses. Contemporary evidence for this is available, but only just, in period photographs where enamel signs appear as incidentals to the main subject. To the uninitiated observer, the edges and corners of enamels, cropped by successive photographic processes, may seem like pasted up paper posters or painted boards, as in (2), where the cropped image on the right edge is an Ogden's Guinea Gold enamel sign. As such, they might be dismissed as being merely of temporary status. Indeed a proportion of the adverts in such photographs are indeed temporary tin and paper posters.

Social historians seldom recognise when looking at albums of sepia street scenes, that some of the advertisements – apparently 'incidental' elements in architecturally inspired photographs – might have been fixed to the walls as soon as a street was built, and could have remained *in situ* until demolition occurred a century later. This failure to appreciate the robust longevity of enamel signs (in contrast to their more ephemeral 'cousins', paper posters), stems from the virtual disappearance of all *in situ* enamel signs since the slum clearances of the 1950s and 60s, and the erection of bill boards at sites previously occupied by enamels. Very few social historians grew up with the phenomenon of the long-term residency of the enamel sign. Inevitably they perceive all street advertising recorded in old photographs as equating only with their own experience of post 1950 'quick-change' paper posters. They do not appreciate that the population of the five decades around 1910 lived and grew up between house walls permanently bedecked with richly enamelled pictures. These images of wild animals and fair ladies, chocolates and cigarette packs, all ornately decorated and embellished with slogans and homilies, must have been profoundly affecting. For a time, enamel signs were part of the permanent cultural fabric of the urban scene.

1

2

7

3

4

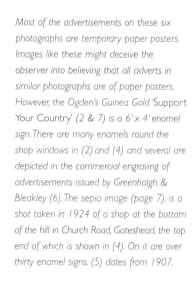

6

5

Most of the advertisements on these six photographs are temporary paper posters. Images like these might deceive the observer into believing that all adverts in similar photographs are of paper posters. However, the Ogden's Guinea Gold 'Support Your Country' (2 & 7) is a 6' x 4' enamel sign. There are many enamels round the shop windows in (2) and (4) and several are depicted in the commercial engraving of advertisements issued by Greenhalgh & Bleakley (6). The sepia image (page 7), is a shot taken in 1924 of a shop at the bottom of the hill in Church Road, Gateshead, the top end of which is shown in (4). On it are over thirty enamel signs. (5) dates from 1907.

Millions of examples of street jewellery decorated towns and villages in a riot of imagery and colour, enlivened by advertising language's purple prose. As such, they acted as a subliminally perceived backdrop to much of the history of the period.

Enamelled iron signs presented paper poster advertising with a serious challenge from the 1880s until the late 1930s. The raw material of their construction, though very much more expensive, was immensely durable, so every enamel sign left in place, carried an advertiser's message and the products' price much longer than its paper equivalent. This longevity was a significant advantage in a non-inflationary era. Both mediums eventually settled into separate niches and co-existed until various pressures exerted by economic, political, commercial and technological forces caused the elimination of enamels. However, in their heyday – the Late Victorian to Edwardian era – enamel signs were a significant element in the mix of advertising media arrayed in the contemporary built environment. Their impact on the lives and sensibilities of the general population should not remain unappreciated and unexplored. The enamel sign was as integral to the lives of the masses at the turn of the 19th and 20th centuries as television advertising is today. Enamels were to be found in profusion everywhere. But they are invisible to today's cultural historians and museum curators precisely because there is no reference point available – absent from the archives, from the histories, from memory. The enamel sign's only remaining witnesses are cryptic dusky outlines on old brick walls – all that is left to show from where they went missing, (1).

Over four decades of collecting and writing about enamel signs we have been able to assess by inference and from observation, the rise and fall in popularity and use of enamels as an advertising medium. The lack of recorded evidence is disappointing but not an insuperable impediment to this assessment. We base our claim for the importance of enamel signs as having greater cultural significance than is generally acknowledged on several criteria:

- dates of currency of typestyles and other stylistic elements;
- fluctuation of market prices compared to those printed on signs;
- contemporary records of when goods became newly available;
- anecdotal evidence in social history;
- demographic evidence;
- database photographs.

Based on these criteria we think that the first enamel advertising signs were produced in the late 1870s / early 1880s. We believe that they promoted products manufactured by leading entrepreneurs (for example Lever's soap, Fry's and Cadbury's chocolate and cocoa), whose success depended on exploiting innovative marketing techniques. Partly fuelled by the 1870s economic slump, and with gradually increasing impetus, virtually all manufacturers turned to enamels as essential to their economic well being. The post WWII decline in the viability of enamels continued until their demise in the 1980s, when what may have been one of the last batches (produced by Garnier's for Irn-Bru) (9), seems not even to have been distributed.

We calculate that the main shopping street of any British town or large suburb in 1935 (when many of the earliest signs would still have been *in situ* and new ones were still appearing in large numbers) would have sported at least twenty enamel signs per every ten shops. Most of these would have advertised confectionery, tobacco products, convenience food, beverages, cleaning products and pet food. On period photographs of street-scenes, we have counted as many as thirty signs on a single shop front (as in page 7). Until all such establishments had disappeared by the 1990s, an average of about five signs could be seen on and inside old shops that had withstood changes of shop fitting fashion and kept their ancient fittings intact.

This book is our latest venture in promoting street jewellery as worthy of being considered as a significant component of 19th and 20th century social history.

1

5

9

A view from my old Bowsden Terrace home (1). The window of a corner shop had been bricked up and black soot indicates where once two enamel signs had been fixed.

This gallery of exotic, alluring, humorous and dramatic images is suggestive of the stimulating nature of 'the people's art gallery' that enamel signs provided (2-12).

2

3

4

6

7

8

10

11

12

Historical background
Origins / historical-social context; a new society defined by commerce

Before written advertising could become an effective merchandising tool, several factors had to be in place simultaneously – literacy, printing, commercial expansion and mass production. These conditions were met for the first time in Victorian Britain.

Throughout history, in cultures as disparate as Maya and Khmer, in places as contrasting as ancient Rome (1) and medieval Paris, religious and state rulers used imagery to impart their 'party line'. Official announcements which were conveyed by public oratory – proclamations in town squares, sermons preached from pulpits – were subsequently reinforced by permanent visual aids, images depicted in diverse media such as monuments, statues, relief carving, painted icons, stained glass and other non-verbal ciphers. Humans have demonstrated visual literacy for over 30,000 years – sufficient time to develop interpretive skills to 'read' the implied meanings encoded in official public art. Although writing was invented some 6,000 years ago, during the subsequent six millennia, literacy has been the preserve mainly of priest and scribe castes. In late 15th century Germany, when the printing press and moveable type began to be exploited, pan-European democratic literacy was enabled. With print technology in place, books rapidly became common-place and relatively cheap. Within a century every European country had its own printing presses publishing a broad range of literature in many languages, including content as diverse as religious tracts, scientific treatises, romances, and political manifestos. Schools and universities sprang up everywhere, mainly for the education of the middle classes, creating a huge rise in the population of lawyers, accountants, academics and other professions depending on literacy and on publications to make their living. By the 1600s, the poor too were beginning to read and write, as the advantages of literacy among the military, the minor civil service and in commerce generally, began to be appreciated.

The first known advertisement in China dates back to the Spring and Autumn Period (770-476 BC). Banners and bottle gourds were used to promote sales in wine and herbal medicine shops. In the 11th century, during the Song dynasty (960-1179), printed poster advertisements and block printing inside products' packaging became popular. A copper-print advertisement for Liu's needle shop in Jinan Province, that includes a picture of a white rabbit pounding medicine with an iron pestle, is an excellent example.

Animal icons, such as the Chinese rabbit, have remained a staple of advertising imagery. The elephant has had currency as a positive endorsement since Roman times, (1) and more recently on the enamel signs on page 15.

Opposite: Elephant imagery on enamel signs from around the world. Examples from India, Austria, Britain, Thailand, Denmark, Germany and France.

1

2

3

This Pompeian fresco (1) from about 47 AD painted on the outside wall of a shop shows felt-makers at work, but also uses images of elephants and a goddess to suggest the strength and quality of their work. Two millennia later elephants continued to be popular visual metaphors among enamel sign designers, and still are in contemporary advertising.

The prehistoric standing stone (2) erected by Bronze Age people thousands of years ago at Edderton, Tain, Scotland, was inscribed much later in about 800 AD by the Picts. Modern scholars are wary of ascribing specific meanings to the kind of Pictish symbols still visible on stones like this. However, it is possible to identify a leaping salmon above the more arcane 'handcuff'-like symbol, which might have held particular significance for the Picts now lost to us. Engravings of a dagger and an axe head on pillar 53 (and others) at Stonehenge may have been markers for the 'pitches' of traders attending seasonal meetings at the site. We are free to surmise that the salmon and the weapons may have been primitive advertisements.

This French enamel jewel (3) of the 12th century extols the virtues of Canaanite grapes.

ON FRIDAY
MISS COMBE
VAUXHALL
HAVE YOU SEEN THE INDUSTRIOUS FLEAS
IS FIXED FOR
TUESDAY MAY 5
JERUSALEM
A VIEW OF THIS BEAUTIFUL CITY
IS NOW
OPEN
SPLENDID NEW COACH!
COMET!
In 24 Hours
LIVERPOOL
EVERY MORNING AT 9
Bull & Mouth
Theatre Royal Drury Lane
GREAT ATTRACTION FOR THIS NIGHT ONLY!!!
MR
HARLEY
MONDAY MAY 4 1835
FRENCH PLAYS
MADLLE JENNY
VERTPRE
THAT HER
BENEFIT
IS FIXED TUESDAY
MAY 10
THIS EVENING!
THE SLAVE
PITY AND PROTECT THE SLAVE
THAMES
TUNNEL
MATHEWS
HOME
Grand Concert
ST. JAMES'S THEATRE
JOHN PARRY
THE SHAM PRINCE
COME VERY EARLY
READ THE
MIRROR!
PRICE 2d
IF YOU
King's Theatre
NEW
MUSICAL FUN
UNDER THE IMMEDIATE PATRONAGE
THEIR MAJESTIE
FRIDA
JUNE 26
A GRAN
CONCER
COMET
ROBERT
PAGANINI
PLAYS
SOLO
THE DESTRUCTION OF
POMPEII EVERY EVNG
E YOU SEEN
HIGH

Legal prohibitions against billposting came about in reaction to the indiscriminate smothering with handbills and posters of every available street-facing surface. By the time enamel signs came on the scene, legislation sought to control this rash of advertising. Enamels tended to be erected with the consent of the owner of the wall upon which they were fixed, thus becoming a more 'respectable' form of product promotion. Of course, to this day, illegal fly posting continues, but as with the examples in this picture, it is an essentially ephemeral medium, advertising current performances, events, and so on., with new flyers quickly obscuring older ones. Officially sanctioned posters and enamel signs erected on legitimate sites tended towards the long-term advertisement of products and services.

To the Victorian mind enamel signs would have had practical and psychological advantages. They were innovative products conceived and born of the age of coal, iron and steam and built to last; literally and metaphorically heavyweight in comparison to ephemeral fly-by-night paper adverts. Enamels had prestige value as well as being eminently practical, so advertisers who invested in them were assured of the added value of what we would now call 'street cred'. Enamels were indeed 'posh posters'.

'A Poster Site near St. Pauls', John Orlando Parry, 1835, watercolour.
Illustration by kind permission of Alfred Dunhill Ltd.

1

2

The engraving (1) of a George Cruikshank caricature shows mid-19th century Eton College 'Oppidans', (senior prefects), evidently having fun at the expense of local traders. It seems that the students have taken the traders' shop signs, and are collecting ransoms for their safe return. Signs (left to right) for a coffee house, a barber surgeon, a grocer (sugar loaf), a pawnbroker, a fishmonger, a boot maker, a hatter, a baker, a vintner and an optician can be seen. Pestle and mortar signs, like that illustrated, (10) can still be seen throughout Scotland.

The practice of mixing heights and styles of fonts in this way goes back to the very earliest printed bibles, continuing into the 20th century, until at least WW1, as can be seen from the date on the Sunderland Empire poster (3). The practice depended on the use of available wooden and metal font sets, some of which might be very old-fashioned. Designers of enamel signs realised that they could use up-to-date fonts and even free-form lettering in imitation brush style, as every enamel sign design had custom-cut stencils, allowing infinite flexibility. Dr. Andrews' Food (5) and Goddard's Embrocation (4) hark back to earlier fashions for the sake of appearing 'traditional' and 'dependable', or were designed before the potential in enamel signs for typeface freedom was realised.

3

4

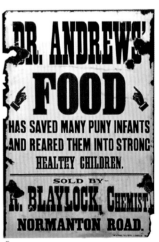

5

6

7

John Thomson's photographs of London street life (6/7) in the 1870s are a rare record of the Victorian underclass.

'Ralph Hedley, Newsboy', 1892 watercolour (8). The picture is 'set' to show the newsvendor stationed near posters promoting the papers he is selling. (Picture reproduced by kind permission of the Laing Art Gallery, Tyne & Wear Museums)

A Virol enamel dominates a clutter of signage on a railway platform (9). The photograph indicates a new environment that burgeoned in the second half of the 19th century to offer a natural home for the newly developing enamel sign.

8

9

10

By 1700, there were sufficient *literati* in most European and colonial populations for printed public proclamations to be posted for the world to read, making town criers redundant; but priests and public monuments retained their importance for a century or so longer. Soon, commercial advantages of the written word to advertise products and services became apparent. The printed word was spread via public notices, newspapers, books and at an early stage, by posters, page 21 (8).

Shops traditionally declared their specialism with carved or painted images of the product that they sold, such as spectacles scissors projecting from the fronts of their workshops. Latterly this tradition was maintained by pubs, pharmacies and pawnbrokers, page 19 (10).

As literacy increased traders realised that their trade symbols could be augmented by adding chalked or painted words, suggesting the quality, type, price and availability of goods for sale. Initially these notices were confined to shop walls and windows, page 20, 1/2/3 and page 21, (4/5/6/7), but before long, ways of distributing written (and eventually printed) posters to the streets beyond the premises were invented. Jobs, like leafleteers, billposters and sandwich-board carriers were created to handle this new type of work and printing continued to develop, becoming ever-more sophisticated. From the mid-15th century there was wooden type. Then followed a range of developments, including etched and engraved words and pictures from the 1600s, then lithography from the 1790s onwards, followed in the late 19th century by photogravure with the emergence of the screen-printed photographic images by the mid 20th century, culminating in the present day, with digital type.

The expanding, literate, waged urban *populus* gradually gained more discretionary spending power, enabling them to buy products of choice, including luxuries, prompting manufacturers to advertise more (page 21: *Slogans Time Forgot*).

1

2

3

This building in Willesden Green shown now and at the turn of the century has part of the advert for white lead, gold leaf and methylated spirit still visible, but the tea rooms advert on the upper storey has been obliterated (1/2/3).

4

6

7

8

*'Ceylindo Tea -
A perfect tea, fresh
grown, artistically
blended, delicious
drinking'*

*'Bourneville Cocoa -
Test against all
others, most
delicious flavour'*

*'Castrol -The
masterpiece in oils'*

*'John Bull Tyres -
Made for the man
who will have the
best'*

*'Topmast sardines -
You will miss out one
of the pleasures of
life if you miss
Topmast'*

*'George's Pills - Have You tried the
certain remedies for Piles & Gravel?
George's Pills Nos. 1,2 & 3 will cure you'*

A mix of painted brick, enamels and other advertising adorn
general dealers (4), showing how enamels were made to 'fit
in' with existing schemes.

In (4) the brick painted 'Fine ales & stout' have horizontal
Colman's starch and mustard signs squeezed in above. Below
the left window a row of small square Fry's signs suggests
that the large horizontal versions were not yet available. Two
Barr's tea signs of different sizes and proportions fit into
suitable gaps, one by the door and one under the right window.

Now faded to near invisibility, advertisements painted directly
on brick near or on the premises of traders can still be found
in many Victorian streets throughout Britain – Newcastle-
upon -Tyne (5), Henley-on-Thames (7) and Whitby (6).

Paper posters and enamel signs vie for supremacy in this
Edwardian street scene (8). The shop is, like many of the
period, simply the front room of a terrace house, using the
normal window for the display of sample goods and show
card advertising.

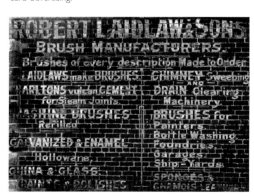

Enamelled cladding on the
Buxton Memorial London
1865 and an entirely
enamel clad office building,
USA c. 1930.

1

2

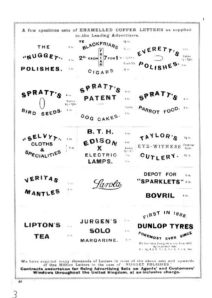

3

These three photographs of EB Jones' grocery shop taken c.1905, give the modern viewer various insights into the shopping experience of a century ago. Facing stiff competition from the drapers/carpet shop next door for catching the eye of the passer-by, Mr EB Jones used every trick of window display artistry, both behind the glass and on the pavement. The 'No wear, no tear, no care' is a glass prism sign, which when viewed from the side would display the name of the product, and when seen from the front would display the advertising slogan.

Enamel signs have a poor showing here. The edge of a Milkmaid sign can be glimpsed, apparently mounted in a pavement display 'A' frame, for the time being (while the photography was being done), folded and leaning against the door jamb. The individual letters spelling E. B. JONES GROCER. are copper foil blisters, white enamelled, glued to the window with mastic, as advertised in the Garnier catalogue for 1907, suppliers of such sets of letters since 1897 (3).

4

5

6

7

8

1

2

The same shop front pictured within the space of a couple of years in the early 20th century (1/2). The family licensed to run the shop has changed and three extra enamel signs have been hung in the later photograph. Some firms paid rent to shopkeepers for displaying enamels. The Burnham's catalogue page (3) claims to obtain advertising space free as part of the contract to produce signs.

3

As with the licensed shop (1/2), Woodward's newsagents (above) changed with the times, repainting 'Stationery & Fancy Goods' on the fascia with 'Tobacconist'. The Macniven & Cameron pen enamel goes, as do the tin Players lifebelts, to be replaced by tobacco specific enamel signs.

There is no single explanation for the emergence of enamel advertising signs at this time. The main spur to commercial and industrial innovation was the Great Exhibition of 1851, which spurred on British manufacturers to win new markets at home and abroad. This prompted the demand for modern, effective and innovative forms of outdoor advertising. Successful experiments with decorated enamel plates as external cladding (page 21, the Buxton Memorial), showed enamel signs would be found 'fit for purpose'. Once in production they gradually gained acceptance, so the enamel sign remained 'centre stage' as an advertising medium for half a century.

The pictures in this section demonstrate the street environment into which the new advertising medium was placed, with an indication of the other forms of advertising that it rivalled, and the 'look' of the streets in which this long-gone episode in advertising history occurred.

In Britain the enamel signs' fifty-year heyday from around 1890 to 1940 was fraught with many socio-political upheavals. Radical politics, successive military and trade wars, burgeoning socialist and feminist issues, all had implications for the advertising industry before and after WW1. Changing fashions in clothes, architecture and furnishing, the development of myriad technological advances from the phonograph to the aeroplane and changing social values, such as increased home and vehicle ownership, all gave opportunities for innovative advertisers to exploit the new enamel medium. However, the pace of progress and technological change fuelled the advent of new media and thereby precipitated the end of enamels as a viable advertising medium. By the 1970s changes in consumer spending patterns and buying trends conspired to turn the long-lived enamel sign into an anachronism. In some areas the fate of the enamel sign was delayed. Enamel sign manufacturing started late in the 19th century in France, Germany and the USA and into the 20th century in Scandinavia, the Netherlands, the Far East, South Africa and elsewhere, as described in the following section. In some parts of the world enamel signs continue to function into the 21st century.

1

2

3

4

Glass and metal advertisements

These painted shutters (5) and coloured glass door panels (6) are survivors of the kind of colourful advertisement display that was typical of the Victorian and Edwardian streetscape. They indicate the milieu in which enamel signs had to compete. Other examples of glass adverts are the Oxo and Dexter signs (11/12). Tin signs such as the Robbialac and Gilbert Rae's (7/13) were used inside and out, but deteriorated due to weathering. Carved, gilded wooden lettering abounded (8), much of it provided by Wildman & Meguyer, pages 84 & 85.

8

9

5

11

6

12

Cartwright & Sons, 219 Cricklewood Broadway, c.1900, with huge step-ladder on the pavement and adverts piled against the wall, prior to being erected, one of which appears to be a Waltham's Brewery sign (2). Already mounted are two Burgoyne wine enamel signs, several large painted wooden panels, enamelled copper letters on the transom window, a lettered awning and numerous posters and packages in the windows. Shop fronts often had advertising as part of the building fabric, as in the Newcastle Breweries gilded glass stall riser (3) and the Knight & Co. game market tiled front in Salisbury (4).

7

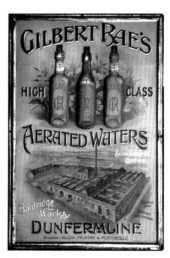

13

The earliest enamel signs are assumed to have been quite primitive in terms of manufacturing technique, design style and advertising content. Sunlight Soap (4), probably one of the earliest, perhaps from c.1885, and Fry's chocolate (11), have the coarse, bumpy enamel surface that was the norm before the chemistry of frits, oxides and metals had been fine-tuned. Pictures 11-13, taken from different angles, catching the light to show the surface contours of the letter edges, show that the white lettering has been applied over the blue. Later working practice had the white undercoat showing through overlaid colour, which was stencilled in negative for the purpose. Close inspection of the enamel surface in (12) and (13) also shows granular bumps on the surface indicative of unsophisticated frit preparation. Cadbury's Cocoa (1), probably manufactured several decades later, has by contrast, a high smooth gloss, evidence that the enamelling process had been perfected. Viking milk (2) exhibits the sturdy, matter-of-fact design qualities and simple two-colour combination of early examples.

Some designs are hard to date due to the use of unchanging logos and 'style-less' fonts over many decades, such as Heinz (6). However, from internal evidence, many signs, like Morriss (7) can be dated with more accuracy. Royal coats of arms and statements of royal patronage provide clues, and anything indicating VR such as Waverley, Pickwick & Owl (10) pre-dates Victoria's death in 1901. The detail of the royal coats of arms is subtly redesigned from reign to reign. The lion and unicorn on (11/12/13) is Victorian, as is the crown on (10) (the VR monogram confirms this), whereas the unicorn having shifted pose in the crest pictured on the Morriss sign (7) shows that the appointment was granted during the reign of Edward VII. 'By appt. to the King and Queen and Queen Alexandra' indicates the reign of George V until the death of 'Alix' in 1925. Few signs were produced during the reign of George VI, due to wartime austerity.

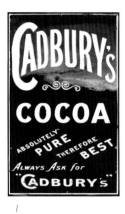

1

2

3

4

5

6

7

8

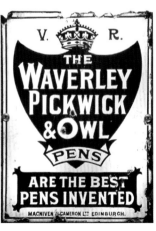

9

10

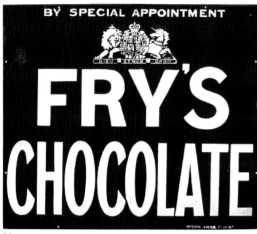

11

12

13

Enamel rivals

The age of enamel signs was also an age of unprecedented technical and scientific progress. In an innovation-led century, the use of domestic gas for street lighting was the first recognisably 'modern' invention c.1803, starting in London and gradually spreading throughout Britain and the world.

Domestic electric light introduced by Swan to Cragside, in 1880, and the introduction of telephones, phonographs, photography, motor cars, high-speed trains, Underground railways, trans-Atlantic cables and so on, with all their countless spin-offs, brought the late 19th century into the 'modern world'. Advertising techniques evolved. Some, like the Ramsay Gas Flashomotor, were even more ephemeral than the enamel sign, while the descendants of the Multiplex swivel-section picture box are still in use. Of course advertisers were cautious about untried methods, choosing to run campaigns using many methods in tandem. The Bigg's Exmoor Hunt cigarette Multiplex and enamel sign are shown here together, but of course thousands of other similar parallels existed.

The 1925 catalogue issued by Alto signs shows examples of translucent coloured panels (presumably glass) illuminated from within by electric light. Bonner signs claimed to be 'indestructible', though their composition is not specified. It is likely that their product was a form of early plastic, possibly celluloid.

The construction materials used by the Brilliant Sign Co. are not specified in their 1939 catalogue, but must be assumed to be some form of plastic, which was becoming fashionable and widespread throughout the manufacturing world, and presented enamelled steel with a real rival for durability, convenience and economy. Brilliant Signs also pioneered the use of neon in Britain, the medium having been first commercially demonstrated in Paris in 1910, and taken up enthusiastically in the USA from 1911 onwards.

The Americans, taking advantage of the same site for colourful advertising displays by night and day, successfully pioneered an

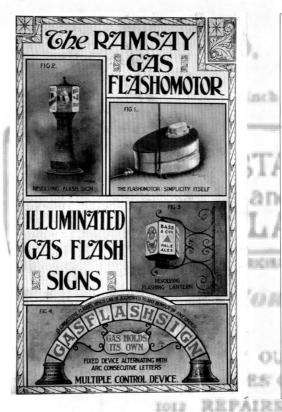

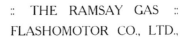

THE RAMSAY GAS FLASHOMOTOR.

This illustration shows one picture on the Multiplex Machine changing into another picture. The change is effected instantaneously.

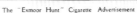

The "Exmoor Hunt" Cigarette Advertisement

REVOLVING FLASH LIGHTS.

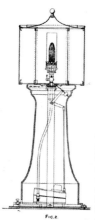

Fig. 2.

IN Fig. 2 the flashing device is shown combined with a single burner and a revolving lantern. The bellows are connected by a connecting rod and bell crank lever with a pivotted pawl, which is adapted to co-act with pins disposed in a circle round the bottom of the lantern, so that when the bellows are expanding under the gas supply, the force of the gas itself is utilised to turn the lantern round an angular distance, so as to expose another side to each point of view. The lantern itself is mounted on ball bearings to reduce friction to a minimum. The movement takes place when the light is turned down.

Fig. 3 (SEE DESIGN ON COVER) shows a similar arrangement for a public house outdoor revolving sign in which the lantern, the "Flashomotor" and accessory revolving adjustment are contained within the lantern body, which is mounted on ball bearings at the top and bottom, to avoid friction from the wind pressure as well as from its own weight.

LIVERPOOL STREET STATION ARCADE
(Metropolitan Railway—Corner of Broad Street)

This illustration shows the general appearance of the Multiplex Machine as erected in Stations, Arcades, and other sites on the ground level.

THE MULTIPLEX ADVERTISING MACHINE Co., Ltd.,
5, Baldwins Gardens,
GRAY'S INN ROAD, LONDON, E.C.
Telephone 5316 HOLBORN. (Holborn End.)

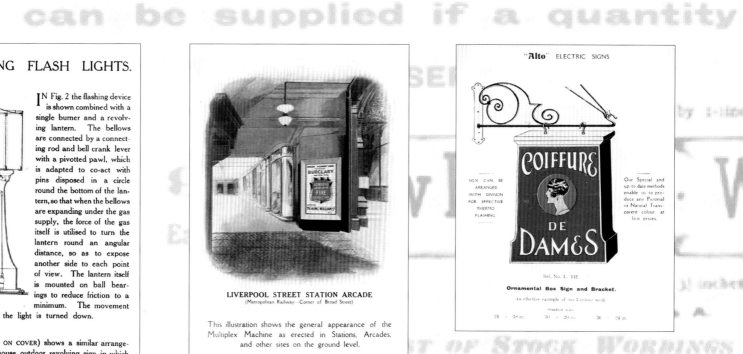

"Alto" ELECTRIC SIGNS

SIGN CAN BE ARRANGED WITH DIVISION FOR EFFECTIVE THERMO FLASHING

Our Special and up-to-date methods enable us to produce any Pictorial in Natural Transparent colour at low prices.

Ref. No. L. 142.
Ornamental Box Sign and Bracket.
An effective example of our 3 colour work
Standard sizes.
24 × 18 in. 30 × 20 in. 36 × 24 in.

"Alto" ELECTRIC SIGNS.

THESE Signs ATTRACT GOOD BUSINESS

Standard sizes
24 × 18 in.
30 × 20 in.
36 × 24 in.

Ref. No. L. 10s.
Box Sign with Scroll Work and Ornamental Bracket.
Advertising Lanterns.

Duplex Glazed 3 Sides.

Hinged Door at Back

Ref. No. 141.
Standard sizes Glass Panels
12 × 8 in. 18 × 12 in. 24 × 18 in.

Standard sizes
Glass Panels
6 × 9 in.
9 × 9 in.
12 × 12 in.

Ruby Panels.
For Post, or can be adapted for Hanging.

Ref. No. 142.

Site Plan of Multiplex erected at London Bridge Station.

Some of the best known Firms among the Advertisers on this Machine.

Wright's Coal Tar Soap.
Worthington & Co., Ltd.
Bazaar, Exchange & Mart.
Prudential Assurance Co., Ltd.
Roneo, Ltd. (Perforated Music Co.)
John Jameson & Sons, Ltd.
N.U.T. Motor Cycles.
London & Lancashire Fire Insurance Co., Ltd.
Autocrat Boot Polish.
White City Garage.
Osram Lamps (G.E.C., Ltd.)
Straker (Sidney) & Squire, Ltd.
Oliver Typewriter Co., Ltd.

Signs for the Times.

This Circular is of special Interest and Importance

TO ALL RAILWAY, STEAMSHIP, OMNIBUS, or TRAMWAY COMPANIES.

Advertisers of Specialities.

IT WILL BE OF ADVANTAGE AND INTEREST TO ALL

Ironmongers, Builders, Decorators, Hotel, Coffee House & Restaurant Keepers. Chemists, Druggist, and all Stores. Tobacconists, Tailors, and all other Trades.

A. M. Bonner Manufacturing Coʸ
8, LONG LANE,
LONDON, E.C.

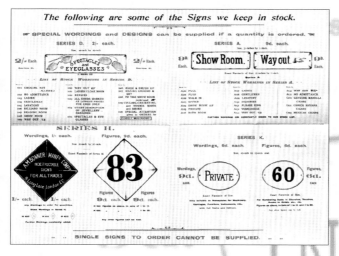

The following are some of the Signs we keep in stock.

SPECIAL WORDINGS and DESIGNS supplied if a quantity is ordered.

SERIES D. 2/- each. SERIES A. 9d. each.

SERIES H.
Wordings, 1/- each. Figures, 9d. each.

SERIES K.
Wordings, 9d. each. Figures, 9d. each.

SINGLE SIGNS TO ORDER CANNOT BE SUPPLIED.

ingenious amalgamation of neon and enamel. It is likely that Brilliant Signs bought in their enamelled copper letters from Burnham, Garnier or other dedicated enamel sign makers. Great store was evidently placed in securing the biggest orders, therefore being the best manufacturer, to judge by pages from the 1939 Brilliant Signs catalogue and the 1907 Garnier catalogue pages 76 to 78. It is possible that the glass pelmets as illustrated in the Brilliant Signs catalogue were made to the same specifications as those detailed in the Burnham's catalogue, which seem to be glass panels.

Product and promotion

The arrival of advertising professionals

Product packaging and enamel advertising

An inevitable event lost to recorded history, was the moment when a trader decided to alter the sign 'Oats for Sale' in his window, by staking his reputation on the product and adding his own name as a 'guarantee of purity'. As long as Jones' Pure Oats for Sale delivered on its promise, market forces would ensure that the Jones business would thrive, and his competitors suffer. This could not happen until the advent of packaged, branded goods in the 1880s, before which all retailers sold groceries and dry goods direct from delivery containers. Herring in barrels, sacked-up flour and muslin-wrapped cheese or blocks and chests of tea were sold by weight on demand. This practice was open to corruption by retailers hoping to make larger profits (for instance, with chalk in flour, candle wax in chocolate). Such abuse led to reform of the system, but meanwhile the public relied on retailers protecting their reputations by selling only reputable goods. For many years, some retailers, such as pharmacists and chocolatiers, had stuck discrete labels on the wrappings of their goods, to identify provenance. But like all other inventions that seem obvious with hindsight, change can only occur when circumstances are favourable and a creative mind is stimulated to be inventive. Pre-packaging, guaranteeing non-adulteration, and increasing shelf life, could only occur when suitable vessels were available. The tin can, the tube, the folded box packet, the screw-top jar, had to wait until technology could deliver mass-produced, affordable items. As ever in this story, circumstances coincided in the mid to late 19th century. The process of folding cardboard boxes was invented in the USA, and the American firm Quaker, were the first to box up their oats, under their trade-mark of an 18th century Quaker carrying a label marked 'pure'. Soon, adverts for pre-packed goods displayed a picture of the package, and a strap line stating that the product was sold 'only in packets'. When price inflation was static, manufacturers set prices in their adverts, protecting consumers from price 'hiking' by the retailer. As well as the specialist technology required to manufacture the various packages (jars or boxes or whatever), further expertise from a new breed of commercial artists was required to create distinctive labels, with added 'selling power'. These artists were eventually commissioned to design posters and enamel signs.

'Snowjob' is marketing slang for an advertising campaign of sudden appearance and high saturation intensity, promoted by every available advertising medium. Hudson's soap company was one of the first to exploit the technique. These images (a framed paper poster and a postcard), from around 1900 are contrived, not documentary, as no single company would have had the resources to 'tie up' every available space on London's bus fleets. However, the images are suggestive of the power of an all-out advertising campaign. The Hudson's adverts on the buses are enamel signs similar to those inset.

Examples of items sold in a 'loose' or raw state, before the introduction of printed commercial packaging.

Barrels and sacks once served both as containers for deliveries to retailers and as containers from which to serve the public. These front and rear views of a tea block, show the divisions on the back that were used by the trader to divide the block into more conveniently small, affordable portions. The honeycomb pattern on the large block of beeswax may have served a similar function. Both wax and tea blocks (sometimes known as caravanserai tea money) measure about 300mm long.

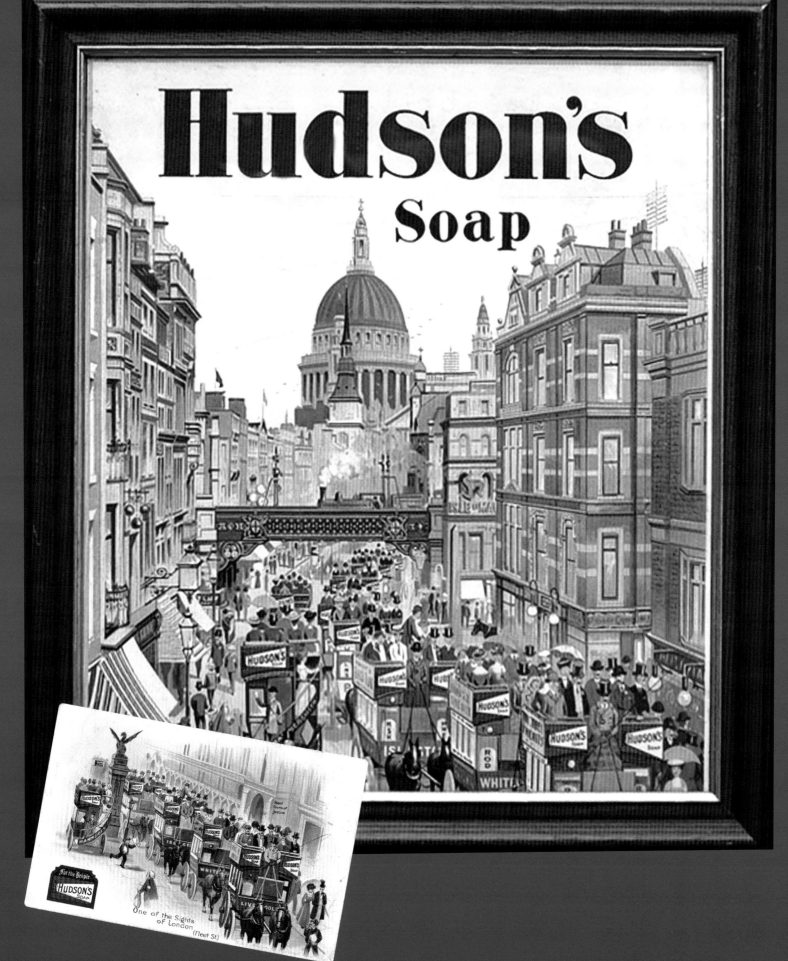

The relationship between client and artist

British artists frequently complained that their names were omitted from designs they had originated. The only names that regularly appear on signs are primarily the advertiser, secondarily the sign manufacturer and occasionally a sign distributor. Only rarely does an artist's name appear on a sign, Hassall being one of the few in this category. European practice was much more in favour of including the designer's name, a practice that harked back to the golden years of Chéret's posters which were much loved and celebrated by publicists and public alike and valued for the personality behind the trade image. Moreover, legal requirements in many continental countries required evidence of provenance to be printed on posters and signs, thus making identification of artists easier. As an example of the off-hand way that advertisers treated commercial artists, Diana & Geoffrey Hindley quote a minor designer, Will True, who complained that, *'Once I did a sketch in which a number of white shirt fronts were displayed, leaving the paper as white as any shirt front, untouched. The advertiser was livid: 'If you think I'm going to pay more than three shillings a poster for white paper you're mistaken, put some pink in 'em''*. The Hindley's add that it was generally agreed among artists that advertisers thought they knew more about poster design than the artists themselves. In an interview in the *Poster* magazine, John Hassall explained: *'The buyers [sic advertisers] are often responsible for a great deal of the bad work seen on hoardings. They are particularly fond of having a figure shifted to the destruction of the composition.'* This latter point comes from a past master of the placing of figures to best effect, as seen most famously in his poster *Skegness is So Bracing*. The generally small-minded and mean-spirited attitude of such clients must have strangled at birth a great deal of potential creativity.

The contemporary view of shopfronts as shabby jumbles of rickety windows and carelessly fixed advertising matter is reflected in this WD & HO Wills's cigarette card and confirmed by the contemporary photograph.

The detail of a wall at the Falkirk factory shows a gallery of finished signs, probably kept as examples and trophies. The steep perspective in the top part of the picture has been artificially stretched in the lower section for ease of recognition of the signs, which include 'Thin cat fat cat'. Reputedly by Hassall, the two 'two cats' signs issued c.1900 are, like the Morse's signs (signed by Hassall), inter-related. They were probably intended to be hung on the same wall, separated by an upper storey window, as in the in situ photograph of the Morse's boys.

Occasionally, Cadbury's produced in-house publications detailing the company's market progress. In 1947 they published 'Industrial Record 1919-1939, a Review of the Inter-War Years', which relates how this typically British, well-established manufacturer achieved success in the difficult socio-political climate of that double decade of the 20th century that included the Great Depression.

In Chapter 3, Marketing and Price Policy, the following reference to Cadbury advertising is made: 'For a long-established business, whose products were well regarded in the public favour and whose name was already a household word, the extreme manifestations of high-pressure salesmanship were unnecessary. The firm's advertising of all kinds was enlarged in scope and improved in quality and variety in a manner which, for the most part, need not be described in detail since the advertising itself will already be familiar to the reader'. Unfortunately, no greater detail is provided and no indication of the past or continued use of enamel advertising signs is given either. However, the photographs, maps and charts reproduced here, give a vivid impression of the ubiquity of general shops in urban areas. By combining the shop distribution indicated by the maps with an average 'sign count' based on other photos illustrated in our book showing full shop fronts, it is clear that advertising of many types, including enamel signs, was a very common feature in British towns and cities.

EXAMPLES OF TOO MANY SHOPS
LEICESTER (CENTRAL INDUSTRIAL AREA)

HULL (DOCK AREA)

SCALE 0   ¼ MILE   ½ MILE

These two maps, each covering an area of under a square mile, one of a dock area in Hull, the other of a central industrial area in Leicester, show the obvious redundancy of confectionery shops. These numbers are based on a survey made before the war.

AN EXAMPLE OF TOO FEW SHOPS
BIRMINGHAM (A MUNICIPAL HOUSING ESTATE)

This map of a municipal housing estate shows the other extreme—the inadequacy of the number of confectionery shops. Many of the houses are over half-a-mile from the nearest shop. The chief shopping centre is on the main road.

● SHOPS SELLING CONFECTIONERY

GRADES OF SHOPS SELLING CONFECTIONERY

25% GRADE 1 & 2

20% GRADE 3

30% GRADE 4

20% GRADE 5

5% OTHER CHANNELS OF SALE

A grading of shops selling confectionery (i.e., chocolate and sweets) showed at least half to be of poor class.

43

OF THE TOTAL NUMBER OF SHOPS SELLING CONFECTIONERY

40% were GENERAL SHOPS
32% were GROCERS
17% were TOBACCONISTS AND CONFECTIONERS
7% were PASTRYCOOKS AND CAFES
4% were selling CHOCOLATES AND SWEETS ONLY

SHOPS COMBINING OTHER TRADE WITH CONFECTIONERY
96%

THIS PLATE IS THE PROPERTY OF R. S. HUDSON, LIVERPOOL.

Paper label glued to the reverse of a Hudson's laundress fingerplate.

Distribution and display

The anarchic behaviour of rival billstickers with their opportunistic philosophy resulted in the piecemeal distribution and fixing of paper posters. From the start of their distribution, enamels were protected from the depredations of billstickers by being located on rented wall space, usually on shops, whose merchants would keep an eye on any attempted incursions of a non-paying kind. Signs would be delivered and hung by the sign manufacturers, or if at a long distance from the point of production by specially commissioned carters such as Pickford's, or by the agents of the end user. Some genre photographs survive to show these activities taking place. Although no enamel sign manufacturing archives survive to

provide information about distribution, the evidence of labels on the backs of signs, a few contemporary photographs, and references in the archives of end user manufacturers, such as Unilever, give a general indication of the process. Batches of signs were dispatched by rail, canal and road to distribution depots or to the premises of end user factories. A small company or in-house distribution system, such as a fleet of horse-drawn drays, would hire an independent carrier to transport signs to sites where they would be erected. There is evidence that Unilever operated in this way. Shopkeepers were paid a small annuity to give over wall space inside and outside their premises for the siting of signs. Sometimes a condition of receiving this fee would be that the shopkeeper should clean and maintain the sign. Some companies, like Hovis, employed teams specifically to tour the country maintaining their signs. As the positive benefits of advertising became more apparent, effort and experimentation was devoted to discovering the optimum use of adverts. WH Lever is reported to have had market research carried out to determine the position of highest visibility and prominence as passengers entered and left a station. By the reign of Edward VII advertising had been recognised as so important that vast sums were being spent. Records show that in Britain between 1900 and 1914, approximately two million pounds per annum was being spent on poster and transport advertising. Examples of individual company spending in 1900 by the soap manufacturers Lever and Pears are, for that time, the enormous sums of twenty thousand and eighty thousand pounds respectively.

Struggle of agents to achieve respectability

The artists' struggle to have their names 'up front' was paralleled by the advertising agencies' ambition to become 'accepted' on an equal footing with their business partners. So prestige advertising, much of which was achieved through the skilful distribution and placement of posters, show-cards etc, included erecting enamel signs at premier sites. An unsuspected boost to the credibility and respectability of advertising agencies came when they were recruited to produce propaganda during WW1. So successful were poster campaigns such as *Your Country Needs You*, (page 000), and *Women of Britain say 'Go!'* that when hostilities ended, the advertising industry found itself on a new footing. This growing respectability meant that there was a new spirit of co-operation between the industry and other public bodies. Even before the Great War ad-men were handsomely rewarded for their efforts. By 1910 people working in advertising in Britain numbered 80,000 to 100,000, often at the high salary of £5-£15 per week. But remuneration

Manufacturers provided copious quantities of advertising material to even the humblest retailers. So, as in this case, accumulations of signs and posters built up in the manner of Kurt Schwitters collages.

To attract the custom of potential cyclists in remote rural communities, Raleigh provided signage in Gaelic and Welsh as well as English.

was not enough. The advertising industry wanted to come in out of the cold and be included as part of the Establishment. One of the gambits played to achieve this was the acceptance by the industry of limitations on where posters and signs could be displayed.

Product specific advertising techniques

In general, signs were distributed to any area of high population density with shops prepared to rent wall space, or transport companies and railways willing to rent platforms, terminus walls, or space on and in vehicles, for display purposes. However, some products were most favourably advertised at their point of sale, so tobacconists, newsagents, sweet shops and other specialists would usually carry proportionately more signs advertising products they sold, than any products that they did not stock. This was of course not a necessary condition, so Hudson's soap, Oxo and Bovril, for instance, were liberally advertised on trams, railways, seaside piers and terrace gable ends. A few imaginative advertisers went a little further, by providing

hardware stores, those that sold soap and petfood, with dog water bowls, advertising Hudson's soap or dog food, to put on the shop floor for the benefit of customer's pets. These and other items of use in the shop, such as dishes, clocks, opening times indicators, scales, maps, thermometers, barometers and door finger-plates were all exploited to the full. Enamel had the advantage of being hard wearing, hygienic and easily cleaned. The famous Raleigh green man on a bike was cunningly distributed throughout country areas, where public transport was thin on the ground and cycling was a good option for those unable to afford a car. Raleigh even appealed to the Welsh and Irish native language speakers by translating *Raleigh the All Steel Bicycle* into Welsh and Gaelic.

In 1909 the Times reports that '*A variety of staple products are now chiefly or largely sold through advertising of specific brands'* and reports that '*over the last twenty five years new inventions had been introduced to the public by advertisement, including type-writers, fountain pens, calculating machines, piano players, motor cars, phonographs, cameras and safety razors.*

Putting a previously 'sold loose' product in a printed packet for the first time was novel enough; issuing enamelled iron signs emblazoned with the packet, and even with the company 'mascot' holding the packet, was an additionally powerful advertising 'first'. Quaker Oats was the first breakfast cereal producer to accomplish this, in 1884, shortly after the invention of a machine that could fold boxes.

The message of universal appreciation conveyed by this set of Quaker adverts is echoed, with a more working-class slant, by the Hudson's slogan 'For the people'.

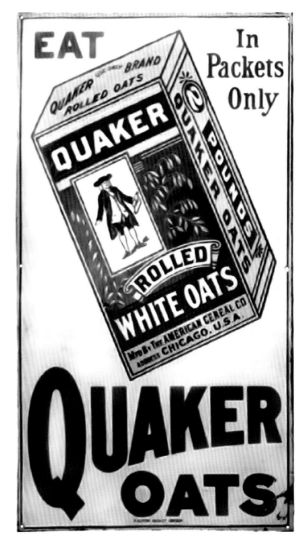

Can 'pyramids' were a standard display technique in 'stack 'em high, sell 'em fast' retail outlets like Lipton and Sainsbury.

A selection of enamel signs featuring packaging

The elaborate displays favoured by Victorian and Edwardian shopkeepers were facilitated by product manufacturers, many of whom provided dummy packaging for window dressing purposes. The cocoa tin towers featured here were provided joined together in stacks along with appropriate showcards and enamel signs which could be mounted inside or outside the shop to complement the rest of the display.

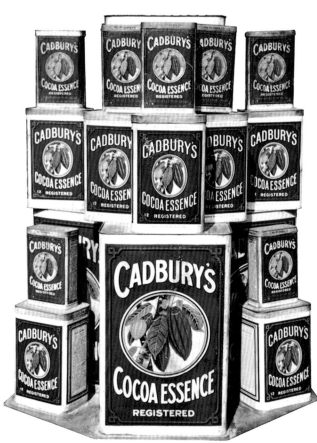

3

2

4

5

6

A possible time progression may be traced through these signs, starting with (9), late Victorian; (4), c.1900 (see also the Cadbury's landau, pages 5 and 128, c.1902; (1/2/3), c. 1920; (7), c. 1925. The text in (9) alludes to the packets and cans, suggesting that similar products are normally available 'loose'. By the time (7) was issued, just composing the sign from the artwork on the can was considered sufficient, with no need of further slogans or even 3D effects.

7

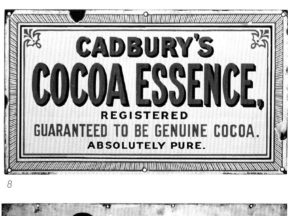

8

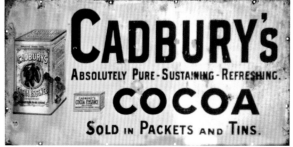

9

1

2

3

4

5

The advertising agents for Bovril realised that its familiar jar profile was an effective advertising symbol without the need for further comment. On this spread are a dozen different ways of representing the packaged product with the support of other text, diverse images and variously coloured or patterned backgrounds.

Before wrapping bread in plastic became virtually universal, brands were recognisable by having their trade name embossed via the baking tin to each loaf, as in (2). Newspapers (14) were also 'self labelled'. Quaker Oats seems to have been the first product to be sold in a printed cardboard box (c.1884), but other products quickly followed suit, examples being (1/3/7/8), or in pre-printed paper bags as in (5). Sealed glass jars, pots and bottles, either embossed with the product name or identified by a paper label were to be found on the convenience food shelf from the late 1850s: (4/10/11/12). Tin cans, which were not commercially viable until the invention of the can opener c.1860, was brand identified by embossing (13), by paper label (9) or by pre-printing the tin (6).

6

7

8

9

10

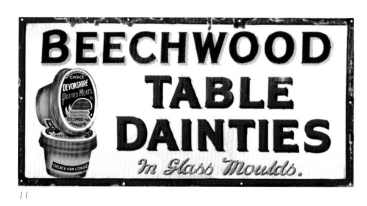

11

12

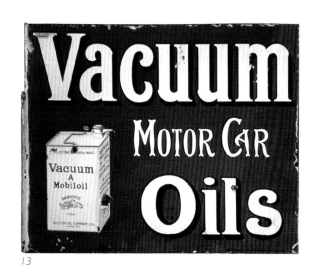

13

14

Hudson's soap

This selection of Hudson's soap signs represents the half dozen or so basic shapes and design formats between c.1890 to c.1930. There were many variations on these, differing in design detail and size. The company established a 'look' for their advertising – curved tops, curly corners (either cut in profile or printed on), a quatrefoil cartouche, a beam of light emanating from a lamp, enigmatic rebus-like groups of letters (see *Transport* for the key to these), laundresses and an arm holding a poss stick are all recurring themes and images. These are always backed up by slogans, including: *For the People, In Fine Powder, Best Value for Money at this Establishment, Established Over 50 years, Used in All the Happy Homes of England, Leaves no Smell.* These long-winded and reverential Victorian phrases contrast with the short and snappy sound bites more typical of 20th century advertese like *For Washing Up and For Cleaning Down.* The exhortation to 'ask for' Hudson's soap is simultaneously as basic and potent as advertising slogans can be.

Examination of most of the signs illustrated in this book will reward the reader with other examples of advertising jargon, but those of Hudson's represent a bench mark for the genre.

The Hudson's soap balloon sign is among the rarest and most sought after of all British enamel signs; it was originally a pasteboard showcard (page 45, 1). The balloon enamel shown on this page is a variant of that on page 53, mainly in the detail on the houses and gardens. In both, there is a tiny 'reproduction' of the curved cornered 'For the people' sign in the lower right corner.

Hudson's 'snowjob' advertising campaign, touched on in the caption on page 32, used as many forms of advert-ising as possible. Surprisingly, Hudson's seem not to have offered chairs with signs on the back like those supplied by Watson's, Venus and Walter Willson. They made full use of clocks (in three sizes), dogs' water bowls, page 48, string tins and tin rulers (page 45, 2 & 3), posters, tin signs (4), showcards, postcards and enamels.

There are many subtle variations of the Hudson's lamp, mainly incorporated in curly cornered signs, whether cut in profile or depicted on rectangular signs. 'For the people' is usually in a Gothic style, but is occasionally in sans serif italic upper case. See page 202 for the key to meanings of the letters on the lamps.

Over many years, Oxo and Virol issued signs that were essentially the same pattern, although the slogans varied: Oxo -white lettering on blue background and Virol white lettering on orange background. They were situated mainly on railway station platforms and buildings. In his autobiography, Peter Ustinov claimed that his mother, when arriving in Britain as a refugee during WWI, was confused by the stations all apparently being called 'Virol', the actual station nameplate totems having been removed as an anti-invasion strategy!

The evolution of the Oxo sign is shown by arranging the photographs in the order in which they were probably issued between c.1910 and c.1930.

Both Virol and Oxo use slogans suggestive of the health-giving properties of their products, the value to children's health and nutritional value of their meat-extract products, even as supplements to other foods such as milk.

Elements that change in the Oxo signs:

- *the shape of the X*
- *the presence or absence of the royal crest*
- *the presence or absence of 'By Appointment'*
- *two bovine heads*
- *one bovine head left and one cube right*
- *one bovine head right and one cube left*
- *two cubes*
- *changing slogans*
- *black shadows on OXO letters as concentric lines or as solid blocks*

Manufacturers & manufacturing

Manufacture: the millennia-old craft of iron working gets vitrified

Ironwork and enamel

Dating back some three thousand years, key sites for the beginnings of small-scale iron working have been discovered by archaeologists at sites in Eastern Europe and Anatolia (eg. Alaca Hüyük). Industrial scale iron working did not occur until the 16th century, when a whole area of Britain, the Kentish Weald, was devoted to timber-fuelled mass production of cast-iron firearms, presaging the huge iron workings that developed subsequently in the North and Midlands, fired by coal. In Europe, the scale of production remained at 'cottage industry' level for a further half-century or so, allowing Britain to take the lead in the Industrial Revolution, with consequent socio-political ramifications of Empire.

Despite Britain stealing a march on the rest of the world, and demonstrating it at the Crystal Palace Great Exhibition of 1851, other countries still boasted particular specialisations. It may have been at the Great Exhibition that Benjamin Baugh noticed examples of German enamelled ware; for it is known that he travelled to *mittel* Europe in 1857 on an expedition of discovery. Certainly, he returned with sufficient 'new' knowledge to start Salt's Patent Enamel Works in Birmingham, and later the Patent Enamel Company in Selly Oak. Enamelling on yellow metal and silver had a long history; it is thought to have originated independently in ancient Egypt and Greece, in ancient China and other oriental cultures, then medieval Europe, notably in France, page 14 (3). However, the enamelling of iron has no ancient precedents, the craft of enamelling (*champ levée, cloisonné*, etc.) having been devoted mainly to the decoration of precious metals as luxury items for church and court. The masterstroke of the German village smiths consulted by Baugh, was to apply cheap silica enamel frit to cheap iron hollow-ware, thus rendering the iron rust-proof with the capability of providing a heat- and water-proof vehicle for domestic equipment, superior to traditional mediums – wood, leather and ceramic, all of which suffer the disadvantage of rapid deterioration or fragility.

A display at the Great Exhibition may have inspired the use of enamelled iron plates for fashionable interior architectural cladding, particularly for ceilings, as in the above example for The Olde Swan in Netherton, West Midlands. This pub ceiling, decorated with motifs, relates to the pub's name. As a 'hygienic' finish, wall and ceiling lining plates were widely used for washrooms, toilets, food shops, milking parlours and surgeries.

Baugh's 'borrowing' of German iron hollowware enamelling techniques may have been to recreate the same processes in England; later to be adapted for decorative cladding and eventually to advertising signs – the pattern of development in later European factories. Hollowware items bearing advertisements – feeding and water bowls for pets, drinks trays and other items such as bain maries – indicate that the same factories that produced advertising signs continued hollowware as at least a side-line. The 1902 Falkirk Iron Company's catalogue includes this photo of a hollowware workshop.

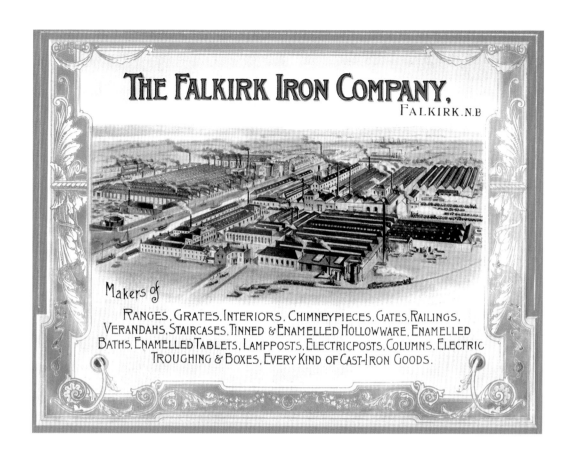

THE FALKIRK IRON COMPANY,

FALKIRK.N.B

Makers of

RANGES, GRATES, INTERIORS, CHIMNEYPIECES, GATES, RAILINGS, VERANDAHS, STAIRCASES, TINNED & ENAMELLED HOLLOWWARE, ENAMELLED BATHS, ENAMELLED TABLETS, LAMPPOSTS, ELECTRICPOSTS, COLUMNS, ELECTRIC TROUGHING & BOXES, EVERY KIND OF CAST-IRON GOODS.

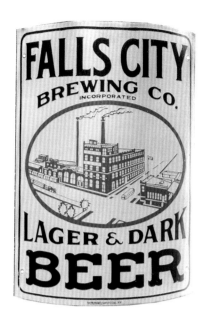

FALLS CITY
BREWING CO.
INCORPORATED

LAGER & DARK
BEER

Anvend til Fodring af Malkekvæg
Sojaskraa
fra
DANSK SOJAKAGEFABRIK A/S
KØBENHAVN.

Anbefales af ansete Landmænd som fortrinligt til Malkekvæg. Erstatter Texas Bomuldsfrøkager. Giver Kreaturene Ædelyst. Højeste Indhold af Protein og Renæggehvide. Tilse at hver Sæk bærer Varemærke og Plombe.

Bergmanns Industriewerke G.m.b.H.
Gaggenau.

Gaggenau Baden.

Her modtages Bestillinger paa Emaille-Skildte fra den tarveligste til den mest kunstneriske Udførelse, efter eget Udkast og Tegning, i to eller flere Farver, fra de mindste og indtil 3 Meter store.

ROWNTREE'S
MAKERS TO H.M THE KING
MAKERS TO H.M THE KING
ELECT COCOA

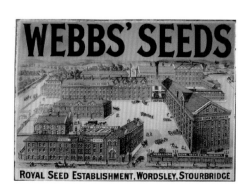

WEBBS' SEEDS

ROYAL SEED ESTABLISHMENT, WORDSLEY, STOURBRIDGE.

Stollwerck'sche Chocoladen

MITCHELLS & BUTLERS

CAPE HILL BREWERY BIRMINGHAM.

Manufacturing in Britain

The Birmingham-based industrialist, Benjamin Baugh, applied for various patents relating to metal fabrication and enamelling processes from 1859 onwards. He wanted to extend the scope of his trade as a sheet metal manufacturer, having visited and investigated the cottage industry enamelling manufacturers in Germany. Patent Office records show that Baugh managed the Salt's Patent Enamel Works at Bradford Street in Birmingham. This firm had a stand at the 1860 Trade Exhibition in London, and secured orders for decorative enamelled sheet iron panels used as interior wall cladding for public buildings. Among the early customers for this product were a railway terminal, the South Kensington Museum (V&A), several churches and some government buildings in the Far East. At some stage during the next two decades Baugh extended the technique of enamelling sheet iron from decorative panels to advertising plates, (page 48). The demand for these advertisements so outstripped that for decorative panels that he began to specialise in the former. The success of this product enabled Baugh to float Salt's as a public company and in 1889 he built a large factory at Selly Oak, Birmingham, customised for the manufacture of enamelled iron signs. This was the world's first purpose-built enamel sign factory and was registered as the 'Patent Enamel Company'. From the 1890s the practical advantages of expanding the distribution of enamel signs were understood by manufacturers and the market for signs had become secure. Therefore the time was right for many independent factories to spring up in Britain and around the world.

During the following two decades it is calculated that at least fifty independent enamelling works were in business worldwide. Unfortunately, little documentary imagery survives to show what these factories were like. Recent finds however, including photographs and other ephemeral records, relating to the Ing-Rich enamelling plant in the USA, and the Scottish Falkirk Iron Company, have cast new light on the subject. Both the Ing-Rich material and the Falkirk catalogue will be examined in detail in section *Design and Style*. The Falkirk catalogue is not a showcase for individual sign designs; it is a record of the industrial enamelling production process. Furthermore the dozen or so 9" x 7" sepia photographs were printed from large format glass negatives, providing highly detailed visual information when small areas of the photographs are magnified. We have made several such magnifications, the source of some images being used to illustrate production techniques.

The Falkirk catalogue opens with an artist's visualisation of the factory site as it might have been viewed from the air. In that era the only aerial views were from the vantage of hot air balloons. Since the 1760s balloon rides had been a dramatic crowd puller, gradually becoming the

1

2

3

The Falkirk Ironworks c.1902
(1, 2, 3) Manufacturing plant. (4) The Design Room.
(5) Cadbury's 'landau' signs stacked on the factory floor, the
original drawing for it on an easel in the design studio. Scenes
of stencil cutting, plate drying, brushing out and kiln firing are
shown; the piled up papers on the plan chest are stencils.
(6) Female workers in the enamelling department. Workers in
the background slushing on grip coat. In the foreground, plates
are carried away to dry before firing.

4

5

6

The story of the Hudson's Balloon stunt

Hudson's sponsored a series of publicity stunts, later captured for posterity on adverts. In 1881, Hudson's sponsored a stagecoach to achieve a record journey time between York and London. Another time, they had their name written on a hot air balloon, which performed a slower, statelier cross-country journey. They marked the event with a magazine insert, show-card and enamel sign. Such aerial views became a commonplace device to provide breathtaking imagery for all forms of advertising illustration. There are several enamel signs on which are depicted such views of factory complexes, landscapes, hotels and so on, drawn not from observation, but imaginatively realised by the artist who combined the skills of perspective rendering with information gleaned from photographs, as in the aerial photograph of Rowntree's factory postcard on page 49.

The Parisian photographer Nadar (Gaspard-Felix Tournachon (1820-1910), who in 1874 lent his gallery for the first Impressionist exhibition, was one of the pioneers of aerial photography using a balloon. The Falkirk catalogue is estimated to date from c.1902, a time when many attempts to achieve manned flight were in the news and shortly before the Wright brothers achieved the first manned powered flight.

focus at events such as elections, other campaigns or public holiday fairs. So, the concept of the bird's eye view was a reality to those bold enough to have made an ascent and the notion had sufficient currency among the wider population for drawings of aerial views to be comprehensible.

The Falkirk Ironworks industrial complex, including all the manufacturing plant and the enamelling department, is shown (pages 50-55) in the greater context of a landscape served by a nearby estuary, seaport and canal, plus road and rail networks. Only horse and steam power are in evidence; no petrol or diesel-powered vehicles are in view. Motoring at this time was in its infancy, being still a private hobby, not yet used for commercial vehicles. More than twenty towering chimneys, belching smoke, protrude above at least a dozen groups of factory sheds, offices, and workshops. The site appears to cover an area equivalent to at least six football pitches.

Photograph 4 (page 53) shows the Design Room staffed by nine men, ranging in age from teens to middle age. All wear business suits and white collars. Each draughtsman is engaged at his allotted task, which in some cases can be guessed at by clues within the picture. The floor beneath the two men on the left of the picture is littered with a confetti of cut paper letters, which are evidently the waste from stencil cutting. (The stencil can be read as 'tea & luncheon rooms'). On the centre tables two youths appear to be tracing from master copies. The three men working on the far bench are engaged in some small scale, fine work, possibly first idea sketches for larger designs, as there are some small designs propped and pinned up near them, and there is a full-scale artwork poster on the wall. Finally, the two men on the far right appear to be making full-scale artwork from which to trace stencils. One of them is apparently engaged on the finishing touches of the Cadbury's 'Landau' sign, the stages of this sign's production can be seen in some subsequent photographs in the collection. Of course, this and all the pictures of workers in the factory were carefully stage-managed by senior management and by the photographer. Nevertheless, there is no reason to think that normal working conditions were any different to those we see in these pictures. The Falkirk Iron Co. was evidently a purpose built, state-of-the-art factory. The work spaces are lofty and well ventilated, with copious natural light afforded by large windows and numerous electric and gas light appliances. There are reports from some ex-workers employed by the Falkirk Iron Co., that working conditions in the enamelling plant just before it closed in the 1960s were among the region's

Louis Ingram

worst. Whether this was due to deteriorating standards, or was always thus, but had somehow been 'sanitised' for the catalogue photographs can only be surmised. Factory owners must have been aware of the importance of having safe work environments by 1900 due to a number of parliamentary debates and pieces of legislation on the subject during the previous quarter century. Less than a decade before these pictures were taken, a scandalised public heard that a coroner had pronounced a verdict of accidental death in the case of a worker who had clearly been poisoned as a result of her job. Harriet Walters of Sedgley, (an ex-worker from

Jordan's of Bilston), who had died an agonising death from lead poisoning, had worked as a brusher out of coloured frit from the cut shapes of stencils. It was clear that lead in the dust raised by the act of brushing had poisoned her. As a result of the scandal, questions about the enamelling industry were asked in the House. In the Falkirk photographs dozens of women can be seen brushing out, with no face mask or other protection. Presumably by 1900, the toxicity of the colouring agents had been eliminated to ensure safer practice. Among the first acts of worker-oriented legislation to make factories less dangerous places to work, were laws to enforce safer working practices in the making of matches. Chemical-based industries, such as match factories, had no regard for worker health and safety. Match girls at Bryant & May contracted 'phossy jaw' as a result of working with phosphorous. Only a concerted campaign of protest by leading feminists pressured the government of the day into legislating to force the industry to change working methods.

Some details are known about the relative status and prospects of designers and stencil cutters from letters sent between Louis Ingram in the USA and his former trade colleagues who still worked in Birmingham and Wolverhampton enamel works. Ingram had teamed up with Richardson to form the Ing-Rich Enamel Co. at Beaver Falls Pa. in 1901. From his arrival in the USA in the 1890s he had found employment with various companies, but eventually, with the encouragement of Benjamin Baugh, had decided to form a company of his own. Using trans-Atlantic mail, he wheedled the necessary expertise out of his former colleagues, who gave up their state-of-the-art knowledge reluctantly for fear of being perceived as industrial spies. One correspondent remarked that stencil cutters were able to sell their skills to the highest bidder, so esteemed was their trade. Elsewhere former colleagues gave Ingram the precise proportions of colouring oxides that needed to be added to standard enamelling frit to gain particular effects, or gave advice about how to ensure good grip when enamelling curved cornered ware.

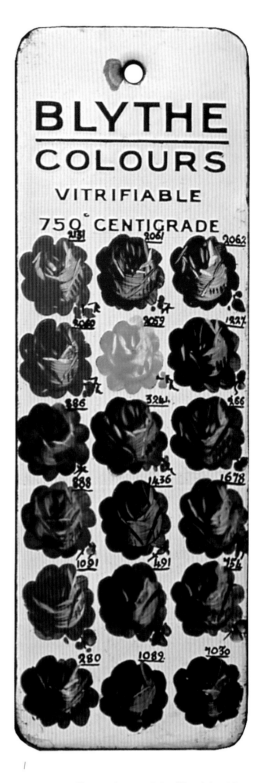

1

This sample enamel sign (1) and the eight issued by Balto (2) show a clear stylistic development from c.1930 to c.1960. (3) Emaillerie Belge, 1987, (4) Escol Products, 2003, and (5) Escol Panels, 1996, are all catalogue pages.

2

3

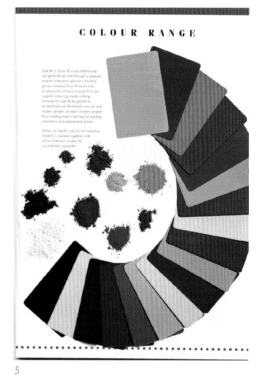

5

4

In terms of enamelling household products, Ing-Rich, Falkirk and Jordan's were enamelling firms which spread their production remit wider than those firms that specialised in signs. Falkirk produced enamelled pots, pans, and baths. Ing-Rich produced linings for early industrial and domestic refrigerators, and reflective panels and housings for electric lights, as well as advertising signs, while Jordan's produced hearth plates, gas stoves and gas fire shrouds, as can be seen from the catalogue pages illustrated on page 62.

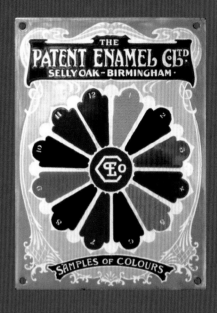

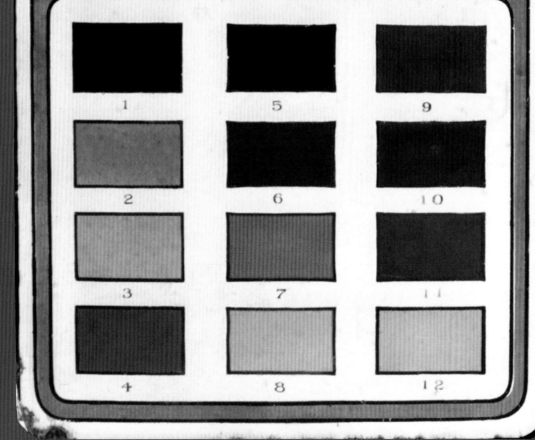

These manufacturers' sample plates both feature Art Nouveau flourishes of a style that dates them to the period immediately around 1900.

When the negotiation and closure of business deals was almost exclusively the purlieu of travelling representatives (so-called 'commercial travellers'), companies issued such travellers with small-scale samples of product as visual aids for use during the 'sales pitch'.

Most of the samples on these pages would have been for this purpose, or to hang in company offices and board rooms. It may be presumed that signs like (1/2/7), bearing the enamel manufacturers' names, were mounted at factory gates and showrooms. The Ingram Niagara Falls (5), the Chromo of Wolverhampton cruiser, page 60, (2), and the Mitchells & Butler leaping stag (3) are examples of the skilled application of lithography to enamelling that would have 'pride of place' in a showroom. The label (4) appears on the reverse of the sample plate (6).

3

4

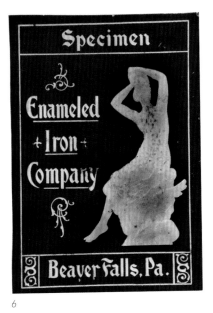

6

1

5

2

7

The trade directory of c.1900 lists (1) enamel sign manufacturers in the Birmingham area. The Wildman & Meguyer entry points to an advertisement on the opposite page shown here (3). (4) is a newspaper advertisement for CE Wilkins, who may have been a sign manufacturer's representative as they do not feature in the directory entry. The cruiser sign (2) is featured centre page on the lower of the two Chromo of Wolverhampton catalogue pages 5 & 6. The magnificent peacock on the Reimbold & Stock promotional sample plate, opposite, shows, in the 'eyes' of the feathers, the range of colours available.

906 ENA—ENG

ENAMEL TILE MANUFACTR.
Candy Walter C. 14 New street.
"Copings, Birmingham;"
Central

ENAMELLED BRAWN TIN MANUFACTURERS.
See Lard Pan & Enamelled Brawn Tin Manufacturers.

ENAMELLED PAPER MAS.
See Paper Makers.

ENAMELLED SIGN MANFRS.
Griffiths & Browett Limited, 68 & 69 Bradford street
Imperial Enamel Co. Limited, 225 to 230 Watery lane
Jenkinson & Co. Watery lane
Patent Enamel Co. Limited, Heeley road, Selly Oak
Wildman & Meguyer Ltd. enamelled iron advertising signs, small door number tablets, enamelled copper letters &c. Sandpits enamel works, Parade.
See advertisement opposite

ENAMELLERS.
See also Cycle Enamellers ; also Slate Enamellers.
Allen Michael & Son, 9 Augusta street
Allison Reginald J. 54 Great King st

1

3

4

5

6

2

Many enamel sign manufacturers started out enamelling items of use and continued to do so when advertising sign production was abandoned. The catalogue pages here show some of the many items from street name signs to protective hearth plates that were much in demand. (1) is the cover of a catalogue which includes (4) among its pages. (2) is a section from a pull-out page in a large Falkirk Iron Company catalogue advertising all the many cast iron products that they made. (3) are pages from a French company advertising their revêtements 'Josz'.

3

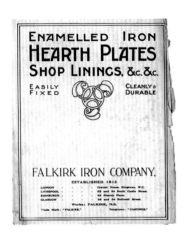

1

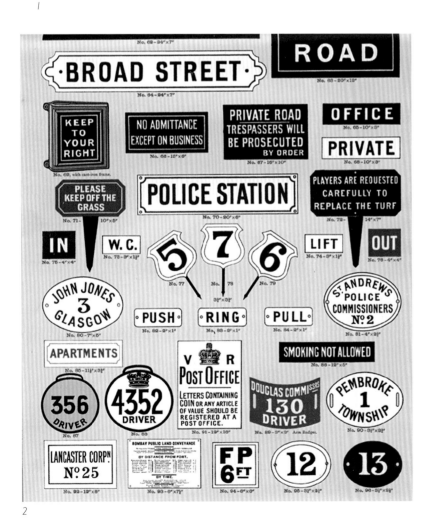

2

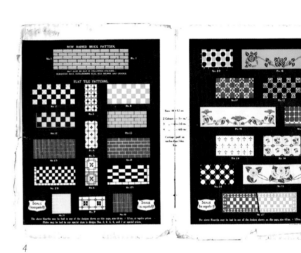

4

5

Like many enamelled iron companies around the world, Falkirk Ironworks produced hearth plates, baths, cooking and heating stoves, hearth fenders, 'splash-backs', interior and exterior wall cladding, lighting reflectors, refrigerator linings, utilities notices, council and other governmental agency instruction plates, house door numbers, street name plates, license plates and many other non-advertising applications for enamelled iron.

Often, advertising signs were a side-line to the manufacture of these utilitarian artifacts. As can be seen in the illustrations here, the impulse to decorate enamelled surfaces with everything from marble effects to Art Nouveau flower arrangements, make many of these workaday objects quite as redolent of their age as were enamel advertisements.

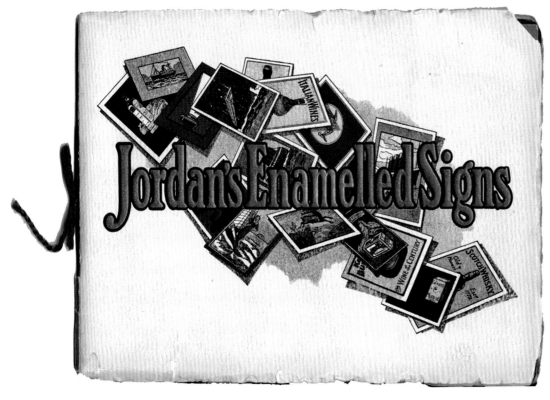

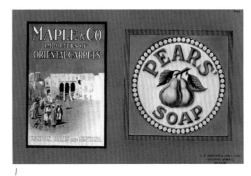

1

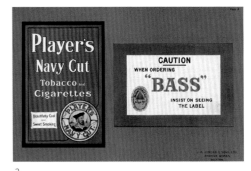

2

3

4

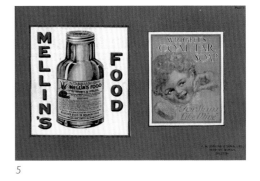

5

6

7

8

9

10

11

MELLIN'S FOOD

FOR ALL AGES

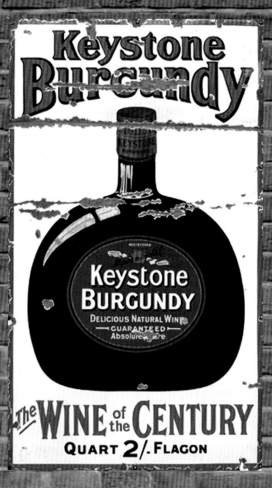

Keystone Burgundy

Keystone BURGUNDY

DELICIOUS NATURAL WINE
GUARANTEED
Absolutely Pure

The WINE of the CENTURY
QUART 2/- FLAGON

Stephens'

THE ORIGINAL
BLUE BLACK
FLUIDS

Stephens' Inks

Odol
The Best for
Mouth and Teeth.

MELOX
DOG FOODS
The Finest in the World

COOPER'S DIP

"PRESIDENT"
THE MOST FAMOUS MERINO RAM IN THE WORLD.
SOLD IN SYDNEY, AUSTRALIA WHEN 5½ YEARS OLD FOR £1680 BRED BY THE HON. JAS. GIBSON TASMANIA,
WHO SAYS "AFTER MANY YEARS TRIAL I CONSIDER COOPER'S DIP THE BEST I HAVE EVER USED"

BEST of ALL

THE
"RAJAH"
CIGAR

2ᴰ EACH   7 FOR 1/-

SEE THAT EACH CIGAR BEARS THE
NAME ON THE REGISTERED STAR BAND

*While we have not been able to locate exact
examples of signs illustrated in the Jordan's
catalogue, we have substituted close equivalents.*

12

13

14

16

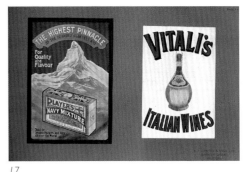

17

15

19

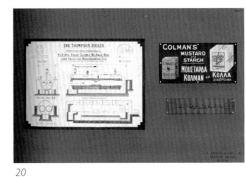

20

18

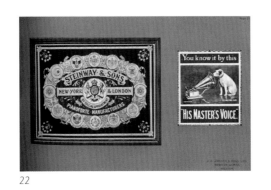

22

23

21

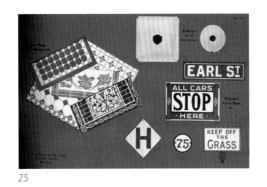

25

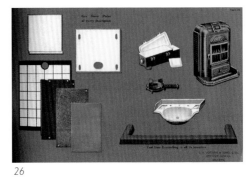

26

24

WHITBREAD'S

ALE
AND
STOUT

IN SPLENDID CONDITION.

QUAKER

PURE

OATS

THE HIGHEST PINNACLE
OF THE TOBACCO BLENDER'S ART

For
Quality
and
Flavour

PLAYER'S
NAVY MIXTURE

Sold in
Sealed Packets and Tins
all over the World

BRASSO METAL Polish

RELIABLE
RALEIGH
Cycles
RIGID RAPID

.You know it by this.

"HIS MASTER'S VOICE."

VAN
HOUTEN'S
COCOA

VITALI

CHIANTI   VITALI   VERMOUTH

ITALIAN
WINES

CARPETS
CLEANED
SHAMPOOED"
SIMTUL PROCESS

PATENT STEAM
CARPET BEATING C
KINGS CROSS.
CARPETS SHAMPOOED
PATENT
STEAM CARPET BEATING C?

Agent for

UP·TO·DATE EXPRESS DELIVERY BY OUR MOTOR VANS
PATENT STEAM CARPET BEATING C? L?
196, YORK ROAD, KINGS CROSS, N.

FOR
COUGHS
Owbridge's
Lung Tonic
FOR
COLDS

*We have been able to find a selection of
actual signs still extant that appear in the
1924 Jordan's catalogue. These are reproduced
opposite the relevant pages.*

or French collectors, Bouisset's Maggi girl is
erhaps as prestigious as Tom Browne's Fry's
o near' boy is to the British. Note that the
rl is holding an enamel sign. In general, the
ifference between British and Continental
gn design is that there are more examples
f illustrated European enamels. These
ictorial enamels imitate the design values of
elle epoch' posters. British pictorials are
nore faithful to enamelling techniques.

Manufacturing worldwide

Beyond Britain, factories for the enamelling of iron and steel became a standard feature of every industrial economy, starting with Belgium in the 1890s, followed by France and Germany, then several other European states by the 1920s. Similar factories opened in some British colonies, as did several in the Americas.

Belgium

An enamelling industry had already flourished in Belgium from the 19th century when in 1838 German industrialist David Moll set up an enamelling facility in Gosselies. By the time Moll acquired Belgian citizenship in 1859 his firm had already become one of the premier enamelling enterprises in Europe, winning industry awards at Vienna in 1873, Paris in 1878 and Amsterdam in 1883. Only items of use such as street name plates, cookware, umbrella stands, medical hardware and so on were produced until in the early 1920s the earliest datable Belgian enamel sign was produced by Koekelburg to advertise the Petre de Vos brewery. In 1923, Emaillerie Belge, the earliest Belgian company to specialise in enamel advertising signs, started production. A law of 1926 which required registration for taxation of advertising signs helps to precisely date surviving examples.

The prominent Belgian manufacturers were Emailleries de Koekelberg, Emaillerie Belge, Emaillerie Howoco, Emaillerie Bruxelloise, Emaillerie de l'Ancre, Email-Chrom, Emailleries Crahait, Emaillerie Leclerc.

Denmark

The Danish enamel industry dates back to the 1840s when, in Copenhagen, Anker Heergaard started to make enamelled kitchenware. In 1886 Carl Lund opened the first enamelling works to produce signs, but these were of the simple informational lettering-only rather than of the advertising variety. Denmark's first pictorial advertising enamels were made in Germany for Ny Carlsberg who ordered 1,000 signs made to represent the Carlsberg bottle label. Until the early 20th century lithographed tin signs, first produced in the 1870s, continued to dominate the market. However, in 1907 the Danish state railway authorities granted a license (unrevoked until 1965) to a newly formed company dedicated to railway advertising, to provide exclusively enamelled advertisements for use on railway properties. Retail outlets soon followed suit, adding enamels to the mix of advertising media displayed on their shops. It was not until the 1930s when the knock-on effects of the global recession made home production of enamel signs economically viable; at this time Glud & Marstrand absorbed Carl Lund and began dedicated enamel sign production. Until that time the Danish market was serviced mainly by German manufacturers.

France

In 1847 the first French publicity agency opened, laying the foundations for organised poster (and later enamel sign) campaigns. When Jules Chéret introduced chromolithography to French poster makers in 1866, he soon became known as the 'Fragonard of the Pallisades'. With significant artists like Lautrec, Manet and Mucha taking to this medium, and establishing a tradition of excellence in advertising design in the 1880s, it is hardly surprising that early French enamels using chromolithography are of unsurpassed excellence. Two of the most celebrated design images from the *belle epoch*, (c.1890 -1914), feature little girls. Both were designed by Firmin Bouisset (1859 - 1925). The first, of 1895, shows a child holding an enamel sign for Maggi in her hands. The other, advertising Menier chocolate, has a child (modelled by the artist's daughter Yvonne), scribbling, *évitez les contrefaçons*, (beware of imitations) on a wall. Major French manufacturers of enamels included EAS, Emaillerie Alsacienne, Bouisset, Ed. Jean, Email du Jura, Email Lyonnaise, Ferro-email and Email du Loiret.

Germany

The original enamel sign manufacturers in Germany were Schultze & Wehrmann (1893) and C Robert Dolde (1894).

Menier chocolate signs from 1898 and 1920 in which the style of the image changes but the message remains the same.

Hungary

Bonyhad, founded in 1907, was the largest enamel works, producing such classics as Dreher chocolate and Unicum liqueur, an example of which can be seen in the background of the factory drawing office, (5). Another prominent enammeler was Brenner of Gyor.

India

India's main cnamelling works was the Bengal Enamel Company of Calcutta, probably operating throughout the early to mid 20th century. Their product is characterised by lively imagery, heavy metal and thick enamel.

Netherlands

Most European enamel sign makers started as hollowware enamellers. Often they adopted advertising as a side-line and then specialised in that field. This happened with Wood & Schraap, founded in 1917, who acquired Keitzer & Bottema, later amalgamating with others to form Langcat BV (United Dutch Enamel Factories).

South Africa

A vigorous enamelling industry sprang up in the Cape Province in the early 20th century, catering for products local to Southern Africa like Joko tea and Assegai tobacco.

Sweden

Swedish railway stations were early recipients of enamels, overseen by the Williams poster company of Stockholm from 1879. Enamelling factories were soon set up by Lundberg in Stockholm, Carl Lund in Malmo, Svea in Vastergotland, Olafstrom in Smaland in c.1887 and Ankarsrums in c.1890.

USA

North America's chief enamelling companies were Baltimore Enamel, Maryland, 1897-1943, Chicago Vitreous Enamel Product, 1930-1980, Enamelled Iron Co, Beaver Falls, Pennsylvania, 1892-1900 (later Ingram-Richardson (Ing-Rich), 1901-1960), Maryland Enamel & Sign Co, Baltimore, Maryland, 1900 -1920, National Enamelling Co, Cincinatti, Ohio, 1895 -1915.

Production techniques

The terms 'porcelain enamel' (USA) and vitreous enamel (UK) should not be confused with the term 'enamel' such as is used as a paint, or 'baked-on-enamel' as on bicycle frames etc. Enamel paints are paints with varnish added to give a high gloss, and therefore an enamel-like finish, while baked-on enamels are merely high gloss japanned finishes cured by low heat and are not in any sense vitreous enamel. Porcelain/vitreous enamel is a glassy composition applied to metal and fused thereon at a low to bright red heat. Although it is a glass, it must adhere to the metal and resist punishment, both by impact and by rapid changes of temperature. This requirement necessitates the addition of other ingredients beside those used in the manufacture of ordinary glass such as window glass, bottle glass, or plate glass. In general, enamel may be said to be a borosilicate of sodium, potassium, and calcium, and sometimes metals such as lead, and zinc. Other substances may be added for special purposes, in order to increase the strength or gloss, or to render the enamel a certain colour.

The three main raw materials for sign manufacture, sheet iron, metal oxides and glass, were bought in from foundries and chemical suppliers. Patent's Selly Oak plant, the Falkirk plant and presumably some of the other companies' factories, had devoted rail sidings, canal arms and on-site stabling that served the delivery and despatch of the heavy raw materials and end product. Ivor Beard's testimony and the evidence of photographs from a surviving Falkirk Iron Company catalogue show that after delivery, sheet metal was treated to become suitable for specific use as enamelled signs. An expensive high grade of iron, pure scotch wrought puddled iron, was the metal of choice until, in the 1920s, Armco produced a grade of steel sufficiently free of defects for the purpose of enamelling. This grade of steel was known as 'vitreous-enamelling quality steel'. Initially the metal was 'scaled' in furnaces, stretched, cut, treated in acid baths and sand blasted to provide a key grip surface. Hand tooling using hammers, rollers and drills followed. Each dressed, cut casting was dipped, sprayed or 'slushed' with a 'grip' or 'ground' coat of a greyish white suspension, the consistency of cream, comprising powdered glass (frit), clay and water. The coating was allowed to dry, stacked in a workshop fitted with steam pipes and then the plates were fired in a kiln at about 900°C. The hot ware was withdrawn from the kiln then coloured frit was dusted on the surface, forming a continuous layer of enamel. The plates were reheated after the application of each colour in turn, but for detailed stencilling or for the application of decals, the plates were allowed to cool so that they could be safely handled. The frit mixture had gum Arabic or cobalt added to ensure adhesion to the surface during the transfer of the plate back to the kiln. This was the stage at which stencils would be placed over a layer of slushed on enamel, and the exposed parts brushed away to reveal the already fired colour underneath. A refinement to brushing was the elimination of the pattern of joining-sprues, which held complex stencils together. This was done 'by eye' and disguised what would otherwise have been an obvious stencil. The gum base burned out during firing leaving perfectly detailed, pure enamel images. The order of applying and firing colours, (each colour achieved by adding metallic oxides to the frit), was determined by the temperature tolerance of the oxide. Oxides reaching the required colour at low temperatures were added last and ideally were added in the sequence of dark over light, black being the final application. Occasionally collectors have found that black enamel applied as a final outline, or finishing tone on signs (particularly on some 1930s Player's signs), is crusty and easily dislodged, probably caused by the final firing being at too low a temperature.

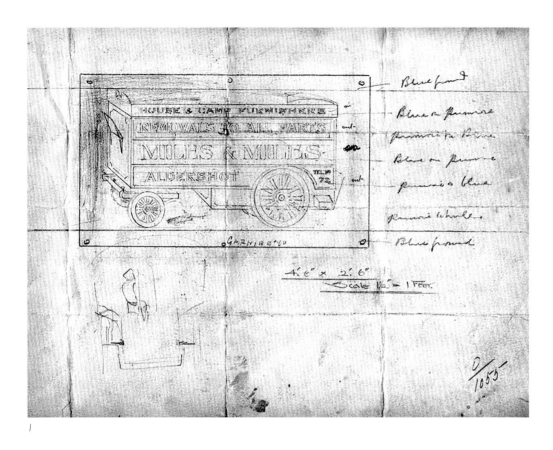

1

Scenes from Swedish (2), Hungarian (5) and US (3) enamelling works. The large roller (3) is being used to ink up a printing plate (4), from which the wood grain effect can be offset printed to an enamel, such as (7). These wood grain effect enamels were intended for use on shop fronts in a trompe l'oeil attempt to match shop front decor. The tiles and bricks on six of the signs on page 150 served a similar purpose. The drawing of a removals van (note the pun 'Miles & Miles') is from the Garnier's archive. It seems to be a generic plan for any firm, like Fitt, needing such signage.

2

3

4

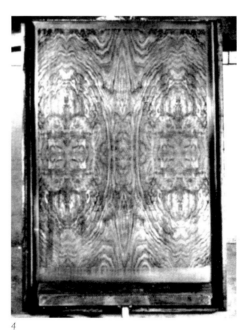

5

6

7

*Pages from European trade press articles
c.1920-1940, featuring German and French
enamel sign manufacturers.*

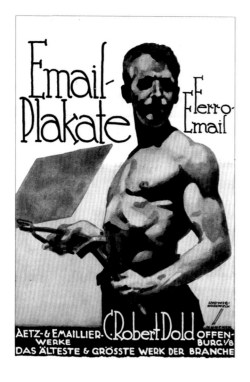

Ausstellungsstand der Firma Frankfurter Emaillir-Werke Otto Leroi G. m. b. H., Neu-Isenburg bei Frankfurt a. M.
auf der Werbeschau in Stuttgart

Torpedo-Email-Plakate auf der Werbeschau in Stuttgart. Die Firma Frankfurter Emaillir-Werke hatte einen sehr großen Stand inne. Er war dominierend in der Plakat-ausstellung. Auf diesem war eine überaus reichhaltige Auswahl von Email-Plakaten ausgestellt für alle Branchen und in allen Formaten, vom kleinen Schriftplakat bis zum vielfarbigen Reklame-plakat von imponierender Größe. Es sind durchweg Plakate, die für Firmen mit klangvollen Namen ausgeführt wurden. Darunter befanden sich auch zahlreiche Plakate mit ausländischen Texten, sogar solche mit chinesischen, arabischen und burmesischen Schrift-zeichen. Diese Vielseitigkeit ist ein Beweis für die weltum-spannenden Beziehungen der genannten Firma.

This girl on an autobahn lay-by is conveniently
posed in front of advertising hoardings with
signs by C Robert Dold in situ.

1

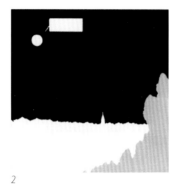

2

3

4

Laying down colour

Stencilling, a method of producing multiple identical images, is an ancient technique, the earliest manifestations of which are the 'negatives' of hands on cave walls, produced by Prehistoric artists (6). Early enamel signs were produced by stencilling lettering through pierced waxed or oiled card, or (for long runs requiring greater endurance), zinc sheets. The detailed images and lettering on modern enamel signs is produced by serigraphy (silk and/or screen printing). Screen printing was patented in France early in the 20th century, and used worldwide by the 1930s. It became standard in enamelling factories after WW II. The sequence illustrated on this page was photographed during the production of a project by Emaillerie Belge, in which a set of Tintin comic strip images was produced in enamel on metre square steel panels (1) to (5). The gradual build-up of separate colours can be seen from this sequence. Occasionally, historic examples of partially printed enamel signs are discovered, like the incomplete Assegai tobacco plate shown below next to a finished, but corroded example (7/8) unearthed from a South African dump!

6

5

7

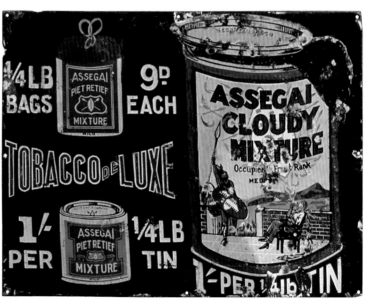

8

Chromographic Enamel Co. catalogue

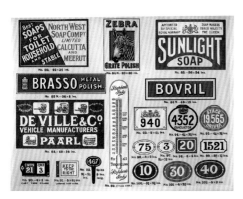

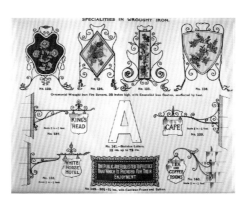

Distributed throughout this book are reproductions of enamel sign manufacturers' catalogue pages. While some of these have been published previously in monochrome, we hope to present a richer interpretation of them in this volume, with, in some cases, complete catalogues and with all (except Wildman & Meguyer's) in full colour.

Names on the edge

With agreement from product manufacturers, enamellers often added their name or logo to the lower edge of their signs. Occasionally the name of the advertising agent (eg. Sir Joseph Causton) or the title of ownership of the sign would appear on the edge (eg. Oxo, Fry's, etc).

The Patent Enamel Company had its factory in Birmingham, plus a sales office in London. The monogram logo is from a very early Sunlight soap sign, c.1885.

Belgian manufacturing tax registrations and dates of manufacture, making all signs from that country dateable from 1927.

Garnier catalogues

Only about half a dozen catalogues for British sign manufacturers have survived, several of which are incomplete or damaged. We have included all that we could access, as many readers will find the fine detail on catalogue pages may yield valuable clues about actual signs in their collections. At the time of writing the only part of the Garnier's factory to survive is the curved brickwork bearing the carved terra cotta name and date shown here.

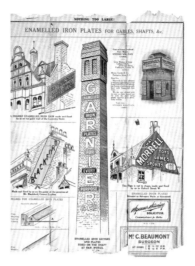

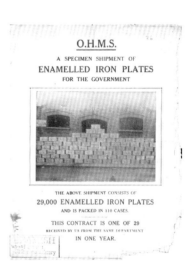

The Garnier catalogues date from c. 1900-c. 1907. Whole and part copies are held by Brent Council libraries local archive and by Beamish Museum, to whom thanks for the provision of scans and for allowing them to be reproduced.

Brilliant Signs Ltd catalogue

The Brilliant Sign Company's late 1930s catalogue shows how enamel signs were produced in tandem with advertisements in several other mediums including back-lit glass, perspex and neon.

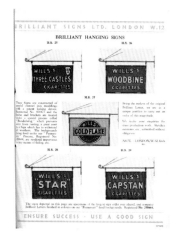

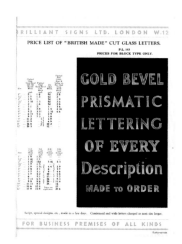

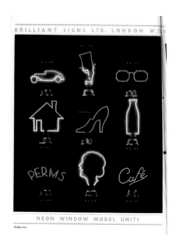

American catalogues

Ing-Rich Signs are used to advertise many well known products in the automotive fields

1	30 x 14	Double Face	Two Colors
2	32 x 12½	Double Face	Three Colors
3	48 x 18	Single Face	Three Colors
4	30 x 16	Double Face	Two Colors
5	40 x 28	Double Face	Three Colors
6	40 x 28	Double Face	Two Colors
7	24 x 72	Single Face Cut Out	Three Colors
8	216 x 36	Single Face	Three Colors

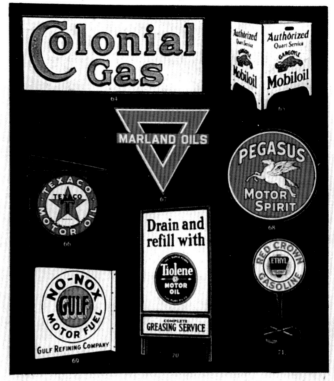

Ing-Rich Signs are particularly adaptable as advertisements of oils and greases because they are so easy to keep clean and attractive

64	120 x 48	Single Face	Three Colors
65	22 x 22 x 24	Cabinet	Three Colors
66	42" Diameter	Double Face	Four Colors — With Rig
67	72 x 72	Single Face Cut Out	Three Colors
68	42" Diameter	Double Face	Three Colors
69	18 x 18	Double Face Flange	Four Colors
70	48 x 72	Single Face	Two Colors—Frame and Supports
71	30" Diameter	Double Face	Four Colors — With Stand

European catalogues

Catalogues are an invaluable source for understanding the 'period look' of the contemporary graphic design fashions that dictated the appearance of enamel signs.

European and American catalogues

The Edmond Jean broadsheet shows a spectacular range of French language Sunlight soap signs plus a selection of signs for Kub, the French equivalent of the Oxo cube.

Famous National Signs

THESE are just *a few* of the Signs we have made for National Advertisers. Yet there are enough shown here to prove the superiority of the Ing-Rich Sign. Signs are an investment. Their only value is their sales value. To post an entire nation involves a great deal of money. You may rest assured that these advertisers would NOT use Ing-Rich Signs if some other Sign returned a higher dividend on the investment.

Made by Ingram-Richardson

SIGNS like these make strong dealers out of weak ones, and stronger dealers out of strong ones. There is no doubt of that. Once more these pages prove it. These manufacturers, representing the keenest business brains of the age, would not spend Millions for Signs if Signs were not unquestionably profitable. And they are just as profitable to the concern of local scope as to the National Advertiser.

The two curved-top signs would have been located at the factory gates of the respective Belgian and Swedish enamel factories, Icopal, Danish manufacturers of roof materials since 1876 and Glud & Marstrands, Danish makers of varied metalware items from helmets to tin boxes.

Wildman & Meguyer catalogue

Wildman & Meguyer's catalogue exhibits an awesome range of shopfront lettering in many materials including gilded and coloured glass, gilded wood and enamelled copper. There is also a selection of enamel signs. It can be seen from the catalogue pages throughout the book that manufacturers such as Fry's, Stephens and Quaker used different enamel sign makers to produce nearly identical enamel signs.

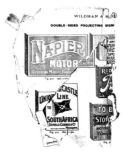

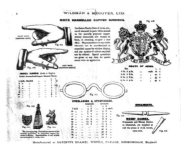

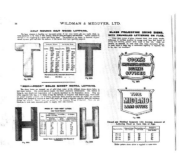

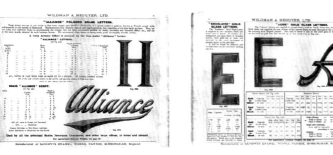

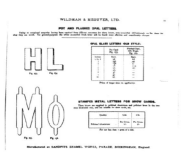

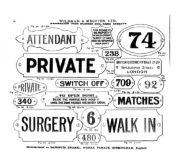

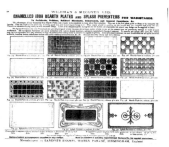

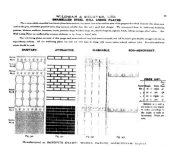

Design & style

A mongrel mix of styles and design traits from other media, eventually matures

The socio-political context of design in the 19th and 20th centuries

As with so many issues, we should not assign modern mind sets to our ancestors. Consumer design awareness as we experience it did not always exist. In the early 21st century, adverts for 'designer' goods assail British shoppers wherever they look, even at each other. We have arrived at a time when people are so keen to demonstrate their discerning taste in the design quality of their possessions, that many people like makers' labels to be provocatively on the outside, rather than discretely on the inside of their clothes and household goods. In a modern design-conscious household, the trade name (turned generic term), 'Hoover', will not do as a description of a vacuum cleaner made by Dyson. A feature of this growing trend is the belief that the 'designer look' contributes value-added quality to manufactured goods. For many people 'design' is as influential in choosing one brand over another, as is fitness for use. This newly emerging perception, experienced by a public with the largest ever disposable income, may have started as early as the 1900s, with support for and commitment to rival makes of automobile. With much the same technology and 'finish', rival automobile marques had to use advertising hype to gain leverage over their rivals. 'Designer consciousness' certainly accelerated with the greatly increased use of cosmetics in the 1920s, progressed to making humble denim smart (from around 1950), and reached a steady stride in all things manufactured by the mid 1970s. The 'head-turning' qualities of designer goods are not intrinsic; they have to be learned. The learning takes place among those 'in the know', who are largely informed by advertisements. Before c.1900, this sort of connoisseurship was an elitist game, the preserve of the wealthy. The *hoi polloi* began to participate because mass production and widespread advertising facilitated for the first time awareness of a specific make of object. The two facilitating phenomena of mass production and widespread advertising had emerged and developed gradually during the two preceding centuries.

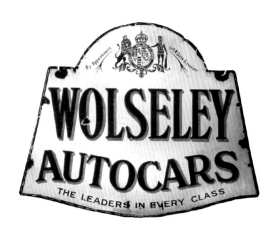

Before the 18th century there were exceptional products made in specific, small geographical areas, or by one particular artisan or artist, that enjoyed widespread admiration. Toledo steel and Palladian architecture are examples of this rare phenomenon. The evolving Industrial Revolution provided far more opportunities for this kind of universal recognition, starting in Britain, then spreading worldwide with trade and Empire. Of the two *foci* for product attribution, one – the more general – was the geographical centre of production, such as the Five Towns for pottery and the Black Country for iron goods. The second was the named individual responsible for providing reliable services (like Clarice Cliff or Viner's). Prior to 1900, very few trade names were recognised throughout the country; among the few (made famous because of transport associations), were Pickfords, Huntley & Palmer and WH Smith. The pride of ownership felt by purchasers of a product by a named, universally respected manufacturer or designer may have been first felt in Italy by Cellini's and Palladio's patrons. In 18th-century Britain, the wealthy young – inspired by their Grand Tours – commissioned homes from Robert Adam and portraits from Gainsborough. At about the same time, (the mid-18th century), less wealthy people throughout the land, whose ancestors would have been unable to afford to own a Toledo blade, could feel proud to own articles of the newly emerging Sheffield made steel cutlery.

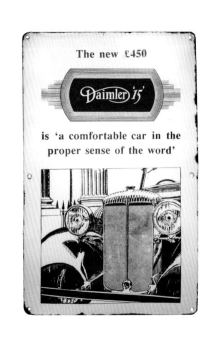

This was unusual and new because from time immemorial to the mid-19th century, most wares were locally produced by artisans, who were usually anonymous or with a reputation only within the vicinity of their workshop. A designer-craftsman would stay in business only if his or her wares were locally accepted as being fit for use. By 1850, road, canal and rail networks were sufficiently advanced to make practicable nationwide safe transport. Thus, regionally manufactured goods like Wedgwood

Every copywriter's dream was and remains to be innovative, to come up with that bright idea that outshines all rivals. In advertising, powerful combinations of typography, imagery and slogan make for creative success, as in this magnificent design, produced by an anonymous marketing firm for an obscure provincial butcher. It is tempting to conjecture that those responsible for this sign may have been aware of and be slyly imitating, the contemporary Daily Sketch 'There first'. In any event, the glamorisation of the saddleback pig – pure pork in a pristine snowscape – is a classic example of British ironic humour, effectively persuading the public to buy with a smile on reading the awful pun, 'First in the field', redolent of Wodehouse's 1920/30s Wooster/Jeeves banter. In his Emsworth stories Wodehouse apotheoses that goddess among Berkshire sows, the Empress of Blandings.

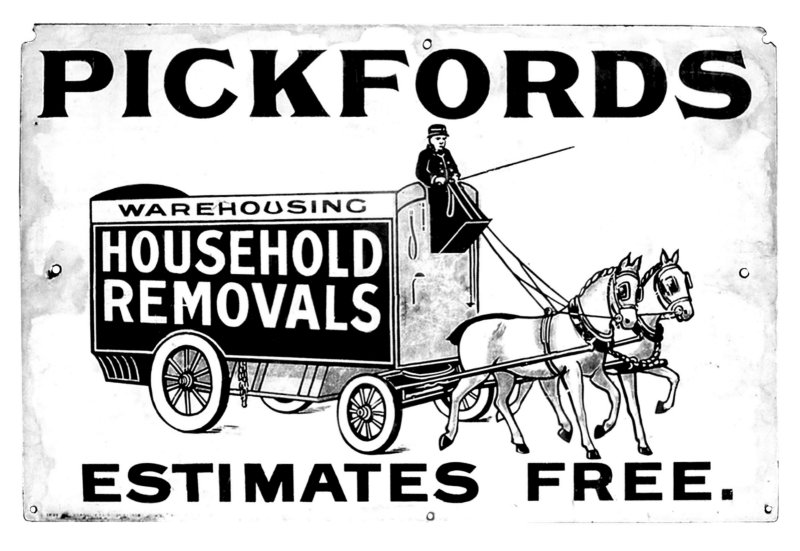

ceramics and Chippendale furniture could be ordered from catalogues, be delivered nationally and become household names. However, not all manufactured goods were of equally good quality as those made by these latter famous names. Many mass-manufactured articles were shoddy, but much cheaper than locally produced equivalents. As the British population grew and shifted away from rural pursuits to factory work in great industrial towns, so a trend of 'cheap and cheerful' retail goods became the norm and whole generations of the working-class masses had no awareness of well designed craftsman-made items that were fit for a lifetime's use. By the mid- to late 19th century, this had become a political, philosophical and moral issue.

Ruskin and Morris - the design watchdogs

The two most powerful Victorian voices speaking on behalf of design as a matter of national importance, belonged to William Morris and John Ruskin. Essentially motivated by their aesthetic sensibilities, the writings and public utterances of both men politicised the character of the applied arts. Both men were born into well-to-do households and had early exposure to the best examples of the 'high' arts, and presumably also of luxurious craftsman-made domestic paraphernalia. Both were passionate about the architecture of their own day and each had expert knowledge of the architecture of the past. They shared a zeal for the improvement of the physical, moral and spiritual lot of the working classes. Both realised that for the masses, one product of the industrialisation of Britain was a coarsening of taste and sensibility. While applauding the contemporary trend of greatly increasing access by the public to museum collections, where examples of good artisanship could be seen, both men realised that every day contact with well designed and carefully manufactured items of use was a more practical way to reach and enlighten hearts and minds. Morris set about attempting to achieve this aim by setting up his studios and retailing goods of his own design and make. Ruskin crusaded for a broad improvement in social conditions and as part of this, inveighed against all the shoddy artefacts and buildings that impinged negatively on people's working and living environments. Morris and Ruskin were just two of the most prominent in a large cohort of middle-class Victorians, including clerics, publishers, industrialists and politicians who held similar views. Neither Ruskin nor Morris approved of advertising. Ruskin deplored anything that did not conform to his narrow aesthetic. Morris was a member of SCAPA, a society set up in 1893 to control the abuses of public advertising. The efforts of this vocal pressure group resulted in an Act of Parliament in 1907, which empowered local authorities to make byelaws for the regulation of hoardings

and the protection of certain amenities. It is an historical irony that some of the best designed, publicly approved art of the late 19th century should be in the form of enamelled iron signs, a medium whose materials and messages Morris and Ruskin would have deplored.

Many social improvers were inspired by the examples set by the British Royal family, notably Prince Albert. In 1840s Britain, the social environment for workers was one of harsh exploitation by employers, who debased workers' lives further by having scant regard for the quality of the consumer goods they manufactured. It is axiomatic of Victoria and Albert that they set an 'improving' lifestyle example to their subjects, who eagerly adopted 'Victorian values'.

On a grander, international level, Albert gave the nation and the world the chance to appreciate the best in contemporary and historical design and technology by mounting the Great Exhibition of 1851 and by posthumously inspiring the Kensington museums, of which the V&A is of particular relevance in the context of this chapter, (page 93).

The taste of the times, in part set by the great Victorians and followed by all who could afford 'taste', was a retro look, specifically a mock medieval style that became known as neo-Gothic. Much wealth, generated by the Industrial Revolution, was spent on hiring architects and builders for the construction of new towns like Manchester and Birmingham, and for the 'improvement' of old towns and old buildings. Morris, Ruskin and others were horrified at the piecemeal destruction or inappropriate restoration of old, especially medieval buildings, particularly churches, carried out in the name of progress (and to sanctify the otherwise dissolute lives of the great industrialists who paid the bills). Unsympathetic tinkering with details from the past, such as supplanting real early Gothic with late neo-Gothic, was a source of great annoyance to the purists. Ruskin and Morris strove to halt and reverse such trends by encouraging truly innovative work. Both abhorred the world's first major prefabricated iron and glass edifice, commissioned by Prince Albert. It was soon to become known as the 'Crystal Palace', the building that housed the Great Exhibition.

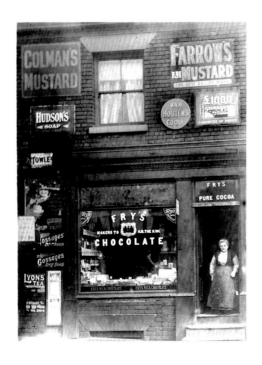

Ruskin's abhorrence of iron and glass as building materials was a typical manifestation of Victorian intellectual extremism at its most absurdly kainolophobic. For every aesthete with prejudices against the new, the 19th century threw up a dozen enthusiasts (usually French) who looked to the future. The ultimate icon for those taking this view was the Eiffel Tower, erected in 1887. The struggle still goes on today as perennial battles between developers, allied to local authorities and their opponents, either reactionaries or visionaries, who despise the standard 'civic project', which is often an inglorious mix of the mundane and the ugly, trampling the old without saluting the new. Matters of historicity or modernity in the content, style and means of production of everything from post boxes to shopping arcades attracted comment, in the 1850s as now, from detractors and supporters who occupied an ever widening pool of 'persons with taste'.

While elite intellectuals were flying the flag of positive discrimination in favour of 'good design', the rest of the population were still making do with what in effect was the lowest common denominator. Advertising was a widespread activity, which attracted all sorts of creative input, nearly all of it from the bottom up. Until 1907, no legal standards were in place and no professional associations or other watchdog groups existed to control or direct the course that advertising took. By the time anyone in authority bothered to look at it, the young advertising industry was well developed and lusty, but without a shred of moral tone.

In the mid-Victorian era morality was a big issue, so when the eyes that informed persons of 'good taste' eventually turned their gaze upon advertising art, they did not like the look of it. One of the problems perceived by the great and the good was the ubiquitous and indiscriminate spread of 'bill posting'. Every flat surface in a street could serve as the support for a hastily pasted-up paper poster. The matter of the poor and 'tasteless' design of the individual poster was not yet really an issue. What seemed to be the trouble was the untidy aspect presented by the riotous jumble of posters stuck piecemeal one over the other, (illustration on pages 16/17 of John Orlando Parry's painting of a poster site near St Paul's in the 1840s and Robson's *Newsvendor*). From around 1900, several national and many local byelaws were passed, to discourage bill or 'fly' posting, both in Britain and other European states. In justification for making and passing these restrictive laws – untidiness being one lame reason – the legislators often spoke on behalf of their moralistic constituents, suggesting that much poster advertising was conducive to depravity and corruption among the lower orders. However, promoters of the medium were unabashed and quite often made insouciant claims for their products being 'in the highest taste'. In its infancy, street advertising was stigmatised as being socially, legally and culturally repugnant. Despite all this, the publishers of advertising posters and their clients, (usually difficult-to-prosecute itinerant entertainers), continued as they still do today, with little restraint. Now treasured by museums and collectors of ephemera, the design and production quality of these posters was poor.

The illustrations opposite display a wide range of typefaces.

The design and development of typefaces

Such design elements as may be found in typical 19th and early 20th century playbills rely on the crude disposition of many mixed styles and point sizes of typeface. From around 1820 decorative fonts, such as Tuscans, Egyptian, antique, Latin, Runic, sans-serif and grotesque by Besley, Caslon, Figgins and others were freely mixed with lighter roman booktypes: *Sunderland Empire 1914*, page 18, (3). The simplicity of their basic 'modern face' style did not inhibit English and Scottish typefounders from extremes of exaggeration when they began to issue display types for theatrical posters, lottery tickets and other 'jobbing' printing purposes from about the beginning of the 19th century.

Their 'fat faces' were soon in demand at home and abroad and developed maximum weight and contrasts of stroke thickness. A typical example of the form sometimes known as 'elephant' was originally cut by Robert Thorne and developed further by William Thorowgood in 1820.

'Egyptian' or slab-serifed types were a logical development of fat face designs, substituting a more or less monotone stroke formation for the contrasting thick-and-thins of the heavyweight modern face romans. The earliest face of this kind appeared in the English founders' specimens between 1815 and 1820. Stephenson Blake's Consort was first issued in 1845. Egyptians were also known as 'antiques', and the lighter (usually condensed) weights as Clarendon. Figgins issued Antique No. 6 soon after 1820. Slab-serifed types with emphasised serif formations began to

appear in the 1860s, and were usually called French antiques. They were extensively employed for theatrical posters in large sizes, often in wood letters, Playbill being a typical example, as in Dr. Andrew's enamel with Playbill type, (page 18, (5)). Reversed types with characters in white on a solid background were first produced between 1828 and 1832, but – from the evidence of the founders' specimens – involved press difficulties, and it was not until the ground was divided up between the letters or hatched (about 1842), that they became popular. In the 20th century Eric Gill issued a version in 1932, which is a reverse of the medium weight capitals that form the basis of Gill's sans family of 1928-1936, as in London Underground enamel, Edward Johnston typographer, (left). Thus by the time enamel signs came on the scene, a wide range of lively new typefaces was available use.

Art in poster design

If the posters were pictorially illustrated it was often with a standard wood-cut image which represented a generic type of event or act, rather than a custom-made, accurate portrayal of the performers. The stakes were not high for a form of art that was largely disregarded by the *cognoscenti*, who considered it unworthy of proper criticism and discussion. If a poster pulled in the crowds, it was doing its job well enough. But as the 19th century progressed, printing techniques more sophisticated than wooden letterpress became widely available. Lithography, invented in 1793 by Senefelder had, within fifty years, become widely used in Europe. By the 1870s the medium attracted geniuses like French artist Jules Chéret.

In 1850 colour lithography was well advanced in England, where during a visit in 1854, the 'father of the modern poster', Chéret, learned the technique. Working again in London between 1859 and 1866 he produced colour lithographic posters advertising theatre, circus and music hall. In 1866 he took the technique to Paris. It was in France where the poster art which he perfected and practised so influentially (Alphonse Mucha, Henri Toulouse Lautrec and

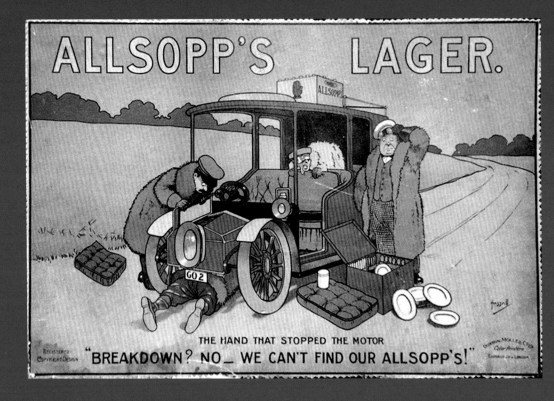

Compare Millais' original painting (centre left) with the two poster versions, modified to promote Pears soap, (centre right and page 10).

Frederick Walker's 1871 poster for The Woman in White, courtesy V&A Museum. Cheret's 1893 Loie Fuller poster, editioned to appeal to early poster collectors, advertised her dance routine.

Posters reflecting opposing moods: Alfred Leete's deadly serious for his classic WWI recruitment poster - in a better known version captioned with Your Country Needs You - and in the light-heartedness of pre-War celebrated by Hassall in his comedy poster for Allsopp's lager.

Pierre Bonnard were his heirs), eventually earned him a Legion of Honour award from the French Government in 1890. Encouraged by Chéret's brilliant example and the enthusiastic approval by French artists and intellectuals generally for poster art, the French made collecting posters a respectable pastime from 1889, with the first exhibition of posters held in Paris being organised by Maindron. Even Manet took up the challenge of poster art with his design advertising Chamfleury's Les Chats. Americans were quick to catch on to the craze for poster collecting, but it took until 1894 for the British to hold a poster exhibition. The first British poster to receive artistic acclaim was *The Woman in White*, 1871, designed by Frederick Walker, a Royal Academician, (page 92). From this time on, with increasing regularity, British poster design began to improve, until by 1900 it was world class.

Sadly, the quality of design achieved for enamel signs in the same period rarely reached the top level. These days we regard Victorian and Edwardian commercial art as entrancing. Whatever levels of quality we perceive with hindsight, our admiration does not equate with the judgement of the time.

For the elite class in Britain then, advertising art of the period (with a few exceptions), was considered by anyone with pretensions of taste, to be vulgar, crude and 'merely' commercial. This antipathy is highlighted by a *cause de scandale* of the 1890s, which was the use as a soap advertisement by Pears of Millais' portrait of his grandson, Bubbles. In respect of this incident Victorian predicators of good taste, like Marie Corelli, made public their disdain for such dangerously *déclassé* crossover exercises between high and commercial art.

No British graphic artist of the time was awarded Establishment honours, which fine artists (usually Royal Academicians) regularly received from 1890 onwards. James Pryde and William Nicholson, used for their commercial art work the *nom de plume* The Beggarstaff Brothers to protect their reputations as 'serious' artists.

Art training in the 19th century

At a less elevated level, the majority of artists who produced adverts of all kinds, were likely to have been trained at one of the growing number of art academies and schools of design that were established from the mid-19th century throughout Europe. A leader among these, in industrial design, were the Royal Academy Schools of Art and Design, which were housed adjacent to the V&A collection for didactic study purposes. Students taking a break from examining exhibits in the V&A might have stopped off at the tea rooms there, where they would have been able to admire the enamelled iron panels that formed the ceiling. The panels, made by Baugh in his Birmingham factory, may well have inspired some young design students to try their hand at industrial enamelling projects. As apprentice artists, graduate students were expected to comply with and to respect the taste and prejudices of their employers and of their clients. Whether neo-gothic, modernist, *quasi-medieval*, or mock Tudor, the fashions of the day impinged on advertising art to an extent through patronage. In the advertising agencies' offices, young bloods at drawing boards 'sneaked in' as much trendy style as they dared. Not all established artists approved of or cared to be associated with advertisements. Walter Crane remarked of advertising art that:

"... there is something essentially vulgar about the idea of the poster unless it is limited to simple announcements or direction ... the association with vulgar commercial puffing (is) against the artist and so much dead weight". Crane's own contributions to the medium seem not to have blighted his career.

The design and production of enamel signs

The earliest extant enamel advertising signs, from the later 1870s to early 1880s, are simple stencilled words, usually the brand name of a product, the name of the product manufacturer, a simple slogan, and a small cartouche which identified the sign manufacturer. This basic

pattern endured as the staple 'house style' for enamels throughout the remaining hundred or so years of their production. The more colours a sign had, the more it cost to produce. Complex pictorial stencils or lithographically imaged decals cost even more. For example, a surviving catalogue of 1888 issued by the Chromographic Enamel Co. offered a four-coloured stencilled lettering sign with small multicoloured central picture and offset coloured medallion logo, overall size 60" x 40", @ 50/- each, 50" x 30" blue on white stencilled lettering only sign cost 30/- each, 50 @ 6/6 each and 100 @ 6/- each. (*Street Jewellery*, page 76 and *Street Jewellery, Revised and Enlarged*, page 86). The relative colourfulness and pictorial richness of any enamel is almost always in direct correlation to the sales volume or high profit margin of the product advertised. The vast majority of signs, for any product, were usually not pictorial or multi-coloured, but were placed just to keep the product name before the public, and to fend off the opposition from prime advertising sites.

From the start, size was infinitely flexible. The largest plate was determined by the capacity of the kiln in which it was fired – usually no more than 6' or 8' all round. However, assembling several plates, edge to edge, on the destination site could create larger signs, (Oxo, page 110). It is recalled by workers at Garnier's that some such 'assemblages' were so huge that they could only be checked for accuracy of edge matching by prototypes being laid out side by side on the road outside the factory. The smallest signs – some just an inch across – were destined not for the great outdoors, but as permanent labels on pieces of industrial or domestic equipment. Ascot boilers for instance, sported a tiny triangular sign in blue and white (page 238). Since by far the most popular destination for signs was shop frontages, the size and format was determined by available space. 6' x 18" horizontal format plates were made for the shallow, wide spaces under shop windows, while 8' x 6" vertical ones were designed to fit the space between a shop door and its adjacent wall. Most common was a 24" x 36" rectangle,

Stephens' Gum

(Strongest Mucilage)

Always Moist
and
Ready for Use

Sticks Quickly
AND
Permanently
Never Ferments

Issued as above at 1/- and in Bottles for Refilling at 6? 1/- & 2/- also in Bell Shape with Cap & Brush at 4? 6? & 1/-. Sample sent on receipt of 2? Stamp for Postage

STEPHENS 191 ALDERSGATE ST LONDON

Stephens
Endorsing
Inks & Pads
for
Rubber Stamps

ISSUED IN BOTTLES AS ABOVE ³/4 oz AT 1/-
ALSO IN 4 oz REFILLS AT 3/- & 8 oz AT 6/-

Measuring · Uninked · Inked
5½ x 3 — 2/6 — 4/-
3½ x 2½ — 2/- — 3/-

Well Finished Enamelled Iron Pads

The Inked Pads
Never Dry Up
and give
Clear Impressions
which
Dry Quickly

Actual Impressions of the
5 Inks BLACK, RED,
BLUE, VIOLET & GREEN
sent on application.

Smoke
Will's
"GOLD
FLAKE"
CIGARETTES

PALMER'S

Always PLANET *Erect.*
PATENT ENDS

CANDLES

VAL
PEPPERMINT
1ᴅ
PER PACKET

TOFFEE
Riley's

The long and the short of it

Enamel signs were designed to fit the available spaces on and in shops, whether around the doors and windows, in the porches or on the counterfronts or shelf edges, vending machines, chair backs and as finger plates, 'A' frames and hanging or projecting double siders. A selection of in situ pictures showing tall thin signs, for a variety of products, is shown here and in the vintage photograph opposite.

capable of having strong visual impact from across a street or at close quarters, when fixed to a wall at eye level. Differences in dimensions were not the only variables that inventive advertisers exploited. Profile shaped, sometimes geometric, sometimes intricately cut in the shape of an object, projecting, hanging, double sided, and pavement 'A' frame variants abounded.

High Victorian, Art Nouveau and subsequent styling

British and American enamel signs rarely carry dates, whereas in Europe ordinances in several countries ensured that origination details be printed on all publicly displayed texts. To fix the age of undated examples requires comparison with stylistically similar, dateable items. As in archaeological practice, comparisons can be made between undated enamel signs and securely dated artefacts that exhibit similar prevailing characteristics, or other date-specific styles. As with fingerprints, when sufficient points of similarity are isolated, the identity is confirmed, or in this case, a means of attributing a production period is provided.

In this respect, it is useful that design fashions have limited life spans. Members of Victorian and Edwardian high society managed – by controlling their couturiers – to avoid the potential embarrassment of turning up to a social occasion in an outfit not *à la mode*. The socially elite beaus and belles insisted that fashion changes take place predictably, on a seasonal basis. Thus sanctioned by top-end consumers, outfits were encoded in and broadcast by the fashion plates of periodicals, making universal fashion compliance possible. Other designers took their cue from this practice, so (securely dated) 'house & home' style journals and magazines often carry illustrations of products advertised. These being similar in design to some enamels, enthusiasts who care to do the research, can narrow the date.

The defining of styles

Fashions in consumables are longer lived than couture, while building, vehicle and typeface styles endure longer, but they also go out of style for longer. One estimate for the 'turnaround' of clothing fashions is thirty years reducing by five years in sixty. Fashion revival in consumables usually takes longer – sometimes centuries. There have been periods when enthusiasm for specific foreign styles has been in vogue. When foreign influence comes to bear on style, sometimes it is by one contemporary culture imitating another, such as when West copied East in the European style known as Chinoiserie of the 1720s and the European / North American style known as Japonnaiserie of the 1880s. But occasionally it is the style of an historical epoch, such as Ancient Egypt, that is the inspiration. Classical Greece and Rome have inspired several neo-Classical movements from the Renaissance onwards, so that buildings with the appearance of ancient Greek temples can be seen on every continent in the last two hundred years. Sometimes countries re-visit their own earlier national trends for the sake of pride in tradition. Examples of this are the several revivals in Britain of earlier styles. Tudor, Jacobean and Georgian originals all spawned revivals in subsequent centuries. All of these revivals are quite precisely recognisable and dateable.

The period covered by enamel signs, effectively the hundred years or so from the 1880s onwards, saw a dozen major and minor period styles come and go. To a certain extent these, like all styles, can be traced to some sort of precursor. Some were original, while others were unashamedly revivals of earlier styles, or imitations of historical or foreign examples. The table on page 102 illustrates with contemporary enamel signs, giving their names, dates, formal and decorative characteristics, associated imagery, typical fonts and patterns in each style, plus historically bracketed marketing straplines.

Enamel signs were designed to last a long time, therefore advertisers of products with a built-in tendency to appear old fashioned, usually opted for ephemeral paper posters. The Fiedler Modehaus sign will quickly have 'dated', whereas the Player's Navy Cut remained relevant for decades. Pages 102-103 demonstrate the way enamel signs reflect the design fashions of the day.

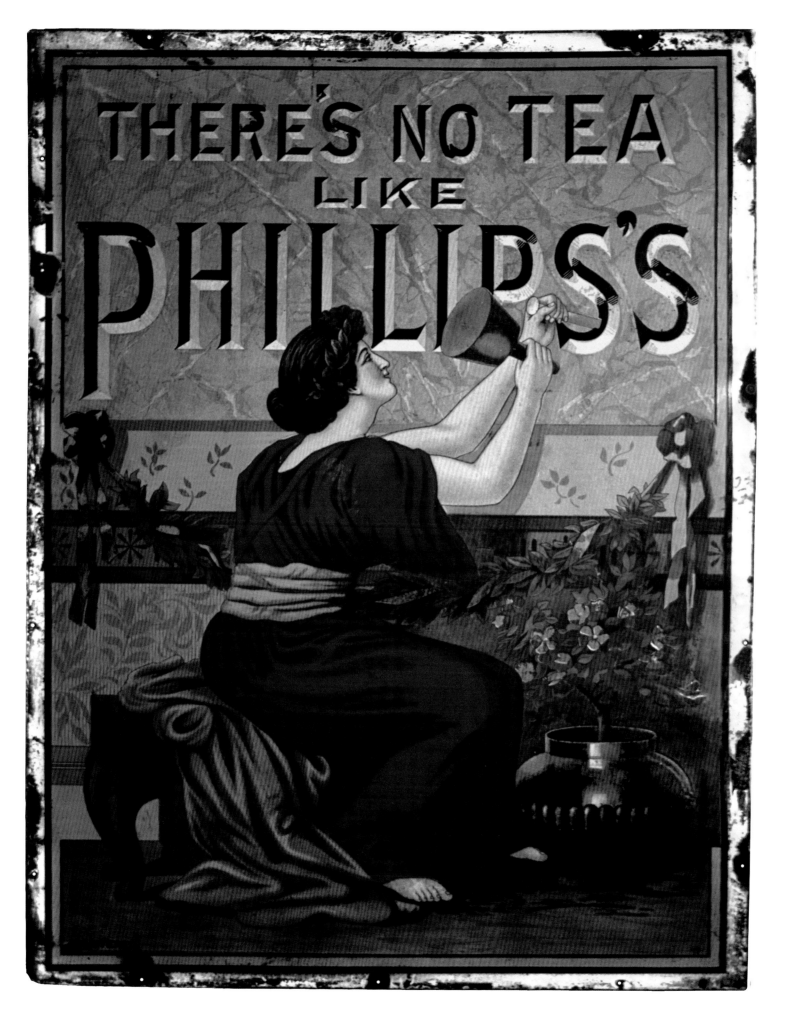

The rise of British graphic artists

The genre of the enamelled iron advertising sign is a perfect example of the marriage of Victorian art and industry. It combines state of the art technology with *avant garde* graphic design. The Great Exhibition of 1851 inspired manufacturers to take seriously the aesthetic qualities of goods that they produced. Subsequent international exhibitions, the emergence of sympathetic commercial outlets like Morris & Co, Tiffany and Liberty, and the associated evolution of the Aesthetic Movement, created circumstances that combined to strengthen this new vision of manufacturing quality. The emergence of Arts and Crafts and Art Nouveau were all part of the process, and are well known and understood.

The socially improving ideals of Ruskin and Morris as applied to art and industry may have reached many middle-class households, but tended to by-pass the homes of the proletariat. Not every Victorian and Edwardian dwelling was graced by Tiffany lamps and Morris wallpaper. Few kitchens sported a Christopher Dresser teapot. Average cinemagoers were less likely to see Loïe Fuller do her butterfly dance than to watch a movie of trains arriving at a station. Full democratisation of the cream of art and design can only be an aspiration. The spread of high quality artefacts is partial and gradual. The exception to this rule was advertising design, the best of which, (like the worst) became available to all classes equally simultaneously.

In the late 19th century art schools opened throughout the country, the London Central School of Arts and Crafts being one of the first in 1896. These establishments proved to be a great encouragement to young graphic artists.

Two new publications provided further inspiration. *The Studio* magazine, launched in 1893, informed art lovers young and old about the latest developments, including the work of Aubrey Beardsley, who gained fame for his contributions to *The Yellow Book*, the quintessential literary journal of the era, first published in 1894. Beardsley's distinctive black and white

The inclusion of stereotypical and/or clichéd imagery, such as the pointing finger (originating from the archaic finger post signage), became scarcer as the 20th century progressed, and graphic artists became more interested in originality.

Don Quixote by the Beggarstaff Brothers. The poster is remarkable not only for its freedom from busy typography, but also for the unconventional square format.

(Left) A Gaiety Girl by Dudley Hardy. These three versions; one pasted on a London street poster hoarding (the colour image superimposed over the original photograph of a poster similar in all respects but for the performance location, at Daly's Theatre); the other two, inset, issued as small-scale collectors' editions.

Hardy's work is shown alongside more conventional pictorial images, and some 'straight' letterpress posters.

graphic style is obviously imitated by the anonymous artist of the P. & R. Hay enamel sign (page 102). The amazing body of work achieved in Beardsley's brief career certainly influenced others of his generation. Between 1894 and 1899, The Beggarstaff Bros issued a dozen or so images that influenced British graphic art throughout the following half century. One of these, the Rowntree's *Three Generations* holds the distinction of having been both a paper poster and an enamel sign (pages 108 & 131).

Brilliant, but less well-known artists like John Hassall and Dudley Hardy, having trained in France, introduced the Chéret tradition to British magazine and poster art. The work of Frederick Walker, Hardy, and the Beggarstaffs transformed the traditional 'look' of theatre posters. The traditional dull column of text was abandoned in favour of a strong and lively pictorial image, supported by the very minimum of text. At a stroke, all other advertising either went with this modern look, or hung back, in a more or less conventional obedience to older forms, as seen in *The Woman in White* (page 92), and *A Gaiety Girl* and *Don Quixote* (opposite).

Typography

Jules Chéret, consummate professional that he was, limited his creative input to the pictorial image only. He left it to fellow professionals to add the necessary typographic elements to his poster designs. Along with Alphonse Mucha, the artist who pioneered the integration of the typography with the main design was Dudley Hardy. His poster for *A Gaiety Girl* 1895, has hand-drawn letters, distributed with no base line, running at off-true angles, inconsistent in size, and with no two 'same' letters looking alike. The flow and space filling quality of the letter, and their 'pattern' is borrowed from the cut and patterns on the costume of the featured dancer. The feel of the text is wholly appropriate to the subject and to the image as a whole. It is completely liberated from the constraints of type-set fonts. The enamel sign for *The Passing*

Show, featuring Lloyd George reading a copy of the magazine, (below right), (dateable by Lloyd George's Cabinet to 1919 -1922), has a similar flair. Although probably not by Hardy, (he died in 1922), the magazine has a cover in *A Gaiety Girl* style. Hardy worked on posters advertising Phillips' Guinea Gold cigarettes during the advertising war between Phillips' and Ogden's Guinea Gold. The anonymous artist or artists who designed the *For your country, Beware of imitations,Two British…*, and *Pleased to see you*, were clearly attempting to challenge his style by imitation. The reason that lithographs could support free-style lettering, is that the whole image, including the lettering, is drawn directly on the stone (later the zinc plate), thus lettering can be twisted, angled, varied in point size, enjoy independent ornamentation and flourishes plus any other unique features that the designer chose to include. This freedom is not available to the typesetter, who must work within the constraints of letterpress technology.

Graphic and photographic representation

The original means of producing an image, either typographic or pictorial, on enamels, in the 1870s when they were being developed by Benjamin Baugh, and right up until the invention of screen-printing in the 1920s, was the stencil. The stencilled image has as its peculiar feature, the contrast between clean-edged areas of flat colour, with no graduated shading or toning. A different stencil is cut for every colour, each stencil being used many times to produce multiple pieces of ware. The strength and durability of the stencil material, which can be made from any stiff, thin, flat material such as oiled card or sheet zinc, determines the number of times it can be used. Texture can be added to the surface of a stencilled sign by several means including overprinting with 'inked-up' decals, (produced by offset lithography), direct brushing and airbrushing. A rough indication of the times when such techniques were introduced are:-
1870-1885: stencilling only;
1886-1899: some litho and chromo-litho details and some direct brushing;

1900 –1919: 'over-all' lithography, especially in countries other than Britain, and the first photographic images. Photographs on early signs were produced by photogravured decals. 1900 – 1930: introduction of air-brush textures. 1930 onwards: screen printing. (Screen prints are effectively stencils with a fine texture held together by the mesh of the screen, capable of producing large areas of flat colour, graduated tones of one colour, or by using colour separation techniques, full colour 'photographic' images).

Lloyd George's cabinet is kept at bay while he enjoys a moment of relaxation.

Printing methods timetable

Moveable type and printing press:
Far East, Korea and China, 868
Europe, Germany (Gutenberg), 1547

Application to enamel signs c.1880

Intaglio engraving / etching
Europe, Holland, c1600

Application to enamel signs c.1885

Lithography: Senefelder, 1793
Rotary lithographic press: Brisset, 1833
Chromolithography: Engelmann, 1836

Application to enamel signs c.1890

Photo half tone: Reutlinger 1897

Application to enamel signs c.1900

Screen printing:, ancient China
First in use in Europe, c.1870
Silk stencil: U.K. pat. Simon, 1907
Squeegee: U.S.A. pat., 1910

Application to enamel signs c.1940

Slogans and copy

Integral to the design of any advertisement is the 'copy', whether simply the advertiser's trade name plus the name of the product, or additional text such as promotional slogans, expert advice, comparisons with rival products and so on. All these have to be treated in such a way that the public at whom the information is aimed will latch onto the main selling message. Sometimes a radical decision such as the omission of the maker's name, as in Ogden's St. Julien *Officer & Gentleman*, can be subliminally perceived as an expression of confidence by the maker that their product is so good it is obviously put on the market by them. In this case the public would have instantly recognised the distinctive blue, red and yellow livery that was the hallmark of Ogden's advertising. Their earlier campaigns with snappy slogans were soon forgotten. Here are some examples of sign language.

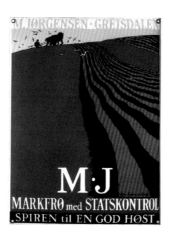

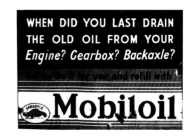

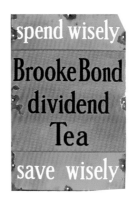

Guide to dating signs

Signs with period characteristics   **Signs with typical formal elements**

High Victorian,
Pre-Raphaelite
Neo-Gothic
1850-1900

Victorian / Edwardian
commonplace
1850-1910

Archaicism / Ancient world
Neo-Classical
1850-1950

Arts & Crafts 1880-1914

Art Nouveau 1880-1920

Art Deco 1910-1940

Futurist 1909-1914

Surrealist 1925-1955

Modernist 1900-1940

Contemporary 1950-present

Historicism eg Jacobean,
Mock Tudor
Old English / Medieval,
German / Early Dutch,
Shogun Japanese / Old West

Ethnic, Orientalist
Mythic, Exotic
1850-present

Signs advertising period products

Signs employing period fonts

Period strap lines / slogans

Guide to dating signs

The preceding table lists several art movements and the associated styles characteristic of each movement. The late 19th and early 20th century spawned more different art styles than had been generated in any earlier equivalent period. Many of these styles impacted on the appearance of contemporary advertising, including enamel signs. Individual signs with strong period 'feel' are, however, rare and thus have particular appeal for collectors. This volume does not pretend to be an art-historical treatise, so the following definitions of the art movements most frequently to be seen reflected in enamel sign design are brief. The descriptions relate initially to style manifestations in architecture and fine art, but where relevant are weighted to show developments in graphic design.

Late 19th century art movements

Victorian Gothic Revival c.1835-c.1870
Enamelled iron signs appeared half way through Victoria's long reign, during a period of Gothic Revival (neo-Gothic) which in 1868 reached its apotheosis with the completion of Sir John Barry's Houses of Parliament.

Characteristics:
Mock medieval (pages 102-103) patterns with details such as pointed arches, masses of decoration eg. sinuous vegetation, fantastical beasts, elegantly formalised folded drapery, furled ribbons, unravelling fonts, etc, references to ecclesiastical art such as stained glass and illuminated manuscripts, and to medieval chivalry and royalty, as in Throne metal polish.

Neo-Classical Revival c.1850-c.1950
The next architectural 'new kid on the block' was a fresh visitation from Classicism, which then filtered down to other design media, including graphics. 'Classical' in this context is a term denoting the imitation of the perceived aesthetic of ancient Greece and Rome. Three distinct classical revivals occurred in Europe and European-influenced colonies from 1400.

The Renaissance, c.1400-c.1600, Classical Revival c.1730-c.1830 and Neo-Classicism c.1870-c.1940. The neo-classicist painters most influential on advertising artists like those who designed Phillips's tea, (page 97) and Matchless metal polish (page 101 were influenced by Royal Academicians like Leighton and Poynter.

Characteristics:
The chief impact of this style on graphics was typographical dependence on Roman fonts. However, classical ornamentation, architectural orders and elements such as the curved arch also found favour in advertising graphics. In painting, attempts to reconstruct the life of the ancients of Egypt, Greece and Rome were occasionally aped as in Phillips' tea and Matchless metal polish.

Engineer Modern c.1850-present
Avant garde architecture of the mid- to late Victorian era was engineer led, dependent on iron, glass and eventually, concrete. Even Barry's apparently authentically gothic stone Palace of Westminster is partially structured in iron.

Characteristics:
The primary impact of this style could not be more pertinent to the matter under discussion, as enamelled iron signs are *inter-alia* dependant on that technology.

Pre-Raphaelites / Impressionists / Post Impressionists / Symbolists c.1855-c.1920 (including early Art Nouveau)
The artists who comprised the Pre-Raphaelite Brotherhood and their followers were non-conformist – in some cases revolutionary, young painters and student artists – who sought to overthrow their professors' academic values. By the time these tyros had themselves matured to become respectable grey-beards, the values of their aesthetic was being challenged on the Continent by the newly emerging Impressionists.

The outrageous image of a gladiatrix, representing British manufacture, defeating another, (foreign competition), in mortal combat. This was perhaps a polite nod in the direction of the Neo-classicists' Roman reconstructions, or an unkind lampoon.

Characteristics:
Pre-Raphaelites 1840-1900, rejected 'dark brown' academicism in favour of 'naturalistic' colouration based on observation of Nature. Acceptable themes: Biblical, Shakespearian, medieval, and contemporary morality.

Unacceptable themes: classical subjects, still life, formal landscape, marine subjects and military history.

Impressionists 1872-1922 rejected pompous academicism, classical and anecdotal subjects; accepted contemporary landscape, townscape and urban popular culture.

Post Impressionists 1875-1900 embraced Impressionist values and in turn influenced and embraced Symbolism, Art Nouveau and Fauvism, treating subjects as diverse as ethnography, magical realism, industrial realism and fantasy.

Symbolists c.1890 engaged with contemporary decadence, including a fascination with Orientalism, overt sexuality, the mystical and (particularly Gauguin) Polynesian culture.

Art Nouveau 1888-1914. The tail end of pre-Modern art, craft and design, being represented in contemporary fashion, architecture, domestic paraphernalia, painting and graphic design. The style (perceived by its exponents, including Beardsley and Mucha, as being very modern), embraced everything from Paris Metro station gateways to films of exotic fan dancing.

20th-century art movements
Modernism
Post-WWI urban societies worldwide gave rise to a style period called Modernism that persisted for much of the rest of the century; (the terms 'Modern Art' and 'the Jazz Age' found currency c.1920). Acceptance by Western intellectuals of the art of non-Western cultures and primitive art on equal terms is integral to the movement.

Also 'new' to fine art was:
- the acceptance of the machine;
- the commonplace object as being of value;
- photography as an artistic medium.

Cubism 1905-1928

Closely associated with Picasso, but also evolved by other artists like Braque and Léger. This is the art movement that not merely broke with, but which shattered the traditional academic art mould. The visual fingerprint of the Modern Age.

Characteristics:

An abstract art form; in painting a means of depicting volume by 2-dimensional representation without resorting to Renaissance conventions of perspective. The Cubists admired ethnographic art and the Primitive work of their contemporary, an amateur painter Henri Rousseau, whose jungle scenes were inspired by the Paris Jardin des Plantes. The impressionists had collected Japanese prints for inspiration; the Cubists collected African tribal and other ethnic art.

Futurism/Vorticism 1909-1914

The Italian branch of Cubism, (Vorticism being the British wing), with a proclivity for glorifying the ultra modern, war and fast movement.

Characteristics:

Shattered picture planes surging with time-staggered images reminiscent of stop-motion photography. The Fry's Five Boys image, arriving as it did at the time when the nascent cinema and the Kodak Box Brownie, (the first practical mass produced amateur-use camera), were gaining an ever widening audience. It would have appeared *avant garde*, being in effect a stop-motion sequence of photographs, echoing physiognomically changing expressions on a sequence of faces on praxinoscope strips, or like a series of film stills.

In the late Victorian period photography ceased to be a scientific curiosity, having been recognised as an emerging art form. Its capacity to represent nature in all its exactitude allowed innovative painters to reject painterly realism and to experiment with 'modern art', including abstraction.

Heine's Würstchen (c.1905) advertised by a flying tin can has a dream-like quality reflecting ideas being explored by Freud at that time.

Dadaism 1915-1922. Surrealism 1922-1980s

German, French, Spanish and pan-European artists' reaction against the militarist nature of the political elite responsible for the World War I.

Characteristics:

Dada erupted as a scream of protest by European intellectual rebels against the triumphalism of the military Powers who had conducted WWI.

Using abusive, puerile, anti-establishment gesturing, Surrealism branched from Dada as its still naughtier, yet shallower, younger sibling, impelled by pseudo-Socialism and Freudianism to *épater les bourgeois* and, as its high priest André Breton put it, '*resolve the previously contradictory conditions of dream and reality*'.

Suprematism / Constructivism 1917-1939

The Soviet branch of Cubism/Futurism, engaged in a fierce propaganda offensive against all things bourgeois. With Dada, it was the most influential of the pre-WWII art movements in re-modelling graphic design and an early exponent of presenting graphics as equal to the other visual arts.

It is a great pity that no surviving examples of Russian Tsarist or early Soviet enamels have come to light, apart perhaps for Singer Sewing Machines, (page 193).

Characteristics:
Minimal imagery presented abstractly in primary red and black against stark white. Primacy of the typeface over representational imagery exemplified in the work of El Lissitzky.

Orphism / Synchronism / de Stijl 1917-1944
A Dutch sub-genre of Cubism whose main protagonist was Mondrian.

Characteristics:
Rigorously demarcated and overlapping colour planes, in the case of Mondrian, divided up by black lines. Driven by a belief that art should strive to create order and harmony.

Bauhaus 1919-1933
The first art school of the modern era, founded by Walter Gropius, whose ethos was to bring art into daily life and to have craftsmen provide affordable well-designed and well-made wares for the public, echoing William Morris's socialist ideals. Hitler disapproved and closed the school.

Characteristics:
The resulting 'look' was a streamlined, chromium-plated, machine-age, cool aesthetic, which is still popular today.

Abstract Expressionism 1944-1980
Combining the total abstraction of Suprematism, the dynamics of Futurism and the hysterics of Surrealism, this movement was the first truly North American art style.

Characteristics:
Jackson Pollock, the movement's most notorious exponent, famously dribbled loose paint (from house paint cans), rhythmically waving the paintbrush to achieve coherent patterns on large horizontal canvases.

Pop Art 1956-1987
The first truly modern consumerist art movement, some of whose exponents were among the first intellectuals to 'pick up on' the, by then, archaic charm and peculiarity of enamel signs.

Characteristics:
Borrowings from the image bank of popular modern culture – the shopping basket, the comic book, the movie, rock 'n' roll, presented with straight-faced neutrality, often using the means of production of commerce and industry, eg. screen-printing. Deliberately 'throw-away', like advertising, as highlighted by Warhol's *'Fifteen minutes of fame'* remark.

The evolution of enamel signs

As the medium evolved, sign manufacturers vied for custom by offering ever more complex, detailed and richly ornamented ware. The technique of chromolithography, developed by the printing trade for full colour images on paper, was successfully adapted for use in enamelling. In this process the sign would usually have stencilled lettering surrounding a lithographed pictorial panel, a classic example being the Fry's Five Boys chocolate sign, (pages 1-4).

The Falkirk catalogue (pages 53, 4) shows a view of the company's drawing office in which a dozen draughtsmen are employed creating advertisements, then converting the original design to a series of cut stencils. According to the evidence of the newly discovered Ingram correspondence, stencil cutters were in short supply in the industry in the 1890s and at that time their trade was among the highest paid. Several signs have survived, some illustrated in the section *Manufacturers & Manufacturing*, produced by sign manufacturers as demonstration pieces for pictorial effects and colour range on offer, to suit the individual needs or budget, of the end user.

The design quality achieved during the height of enamel signs was often very basic. British artists who illustrated adverts were more often than not obliged by their employers to remain anonymous. When John Hassall negotiated the 'privilege' of signing his work, he remained a notable exception.

Sir Alfred Munnings' design for the Bullard's Beer enamel, (page 115, 9) was executed when, as a student, he entered a competition set by the Bullard's brewery. Sir William Nicholson's design for the Rowntree's Three Generations cocoa sign, (top right and page 131) was an early work done when he was still unknown, and even then he and his collaborator James Pryde hid their respectable artistic identities behind the pseudonymous Beggarstaff Brothers trademark. There was low pay and little glory in being an advertising artist. Fees for an advertising drawing ranged from 10/6d for an unknown artist to £100 for a 'name' like Hassall or the Beggarstaffs, with a normal payment of £25. Little surprise then, that few British designers' names can be confidently associated with particular enamel signs.

It would seem that, for most traditional art or museum establishments, a repugnant cloud still clings to advertising art and enamel signs. In the 2000 V&A Art Nouveau exhibition, not a single enamel sign was on display. The distaste was articulated when our first book on enamel advertising, *Street Jewellery*, being reviewed by Quentin Crisp in *The Designer* (September 1978, p.18) attracted this dry observation from the 'doyen of the aesthetic', who could remember them from his youthful days: "*... there is no way in which we can for long keep up the pretence that ... enamel signs were beautiful ... Street Jewellery is an interesting book, but enamel signs were hideous.*" We still maintain, however, that these objects, beautiful or hideous, provided a truly democratic, ubiquitous, free-for-all art gallery that cheered the lives of those huddled masses populating the otherwise bleak urban streets of industrial Britain. It might not have been 'good' art, but it was aimed at raising the spirits. Furthermore, the enamel sign as a genre currently serves as a useful insight to the lives of ordinary British people and commercial practices of a hundred years ago, being now, at the very least, delightful objects to collect and ornament modern homes.

Age, size and makes of signs. Product specific styling

Much in the same way as the categorisation of fine art into landscape, portrait, still-life, genre and so on, helps in appreciating the artist's intentions when creating the image, so can a similar categorisation explain the nuances of 'sales pitch' that motivates commercial artists when producing various adverts.

Rowntree's Elect Cocoa. The Beggarstaff Bros. clearly had the requirements of the 'stencil' driven production process in mind when they designed the Three Generations poster in 1896, later adapted for this enamel sign, another colour-way version of which is illustrated on page 131.

WH Lever was so ambitious, that within a decade of founding his Sunlight Soap brand, he had sales branches in many countries.

Two 'ages' of Sunlight soap delivery vehicles, from horse-drawn of the 1890s, to the motor wagon, first introduced in 1904. Both have a force of sales representatives, who took their advertisments with them. Sunlight soap was one of the earliest products to be advertised by enamel signs, so following the history of Sunlight makes a good case study showing design development from the simple to the sophisticated. All types of sign apart from 'A' frame are represented depicting design concepts, styles and applications from c.1885 to c.1955, pages 110-11.

The Sunlight factory boys holding bags of money may have had three functions: 1. as delivery wagon decoration; 2. fixed flat to walls; 3. strapped back to back, so as to project into the street from a shop-front. Certainly the concept of catching the eye from varied approaches along the street was exploited by the 'optical boards' introduced in the 1890s. These read 'More comfort' and 'Less work' when viewed from left or right. The zig-zag effect of these boards, like many Toblerone bars stacked vertically edge to edge, can be seen in an advert 'No wear, no tear, no care' under the window of Mr. Jones' shop, (page 23). This slogan probably superceded the 'Less labour, greater comfort' inscribed on the earliest enamels (pages 110-11). William Hesketh Lever was one of the first British industrialists to exploit every form of advertising medium.

2 February 1884: Lever registers the Sunlight trademark, and on 19 September, the 'self washer' trade mark. Sunlight is manufactured by other soapmakers until 1885.

1885: First Sunlight advertising appears on northern railway stations. Lever leases Warrington factory and begins production.

1886: Despatching the first batch from there in January. Introduction of soap in cartons and offer of £1,000 reward for any impurities found in the product.

1890: Firm becomes Lever Brothers Limited, a private limited company

1892: Company appointed Soapmakers to Queen Victoria.

1908: Royal warrants for Lever's soap granted by Kings of Britain, Siam, Portugal and Spain, Prince of Wales and Sultan of Turkey. Siamese (Thai) packaging is shown at left.

The earliest styling, employed for playbills, was a tall, narrow support densely packed with text, dramatically shifting between tiny and very large type sizes and font styles. A 'luxury' addition to this pattern was the occasional wood cut image.

With a few exceptions, (page 18), the earliest enamel signs avoid this tradition, leaning towards shop signs identifying the proprietor and / or trade of the shop. Plain text, of one colour against a contrasting background colour, within a wide rectangle, probably designated for placing below a shop window fascia seems to have been the norm.

With growing confidence in the medium, more elaborate designs emerged. Stencils offered more scope to the designer than moveable type. They facilitated the use of more colours and more richly coloured images, thereby enabling the enamel sign to develop its own personality. Experiments with supports in many shapes and sizes, including cut-outs and projecting 'flags', were continuous and varied. Within a decade, specific types of design evolved, sometimes having strong links with particular products.

Sunlight, Oxo and many other signs had identical designs produced in a wide range of sizes. The £1,000 Sunlight was issued in a range from 8' x 4', to 36" x 24". The larger Oxo, left was made in two sections which together add up to 4' x 12'.

The 12"wide counter front sign (bottom of centre column) may be one of the first ever enamel advertising signs, designed to be a reminder in the shop of the larger ones of about 52",(two top signs, left), that sport the same sloping lettering, but additionally have two slogans, 'Self washer' and 'Less labour, greater comfort'. The Lever Brothers Warrington text indicates a date before 1890 when Lever Brothers became Lever Brothers Limited. The customer would have been reminded of Sunlight soap on the shop front under the fascia, on the window (enamelled letters and Royal Warrant), and even when going out of the door, as they pushed on the finger plate, (page 110).

Sunlight soap gained markets all over the world. Signs from France, Germany, India and South Africa are shown on this page. The firm held the market in Britain for decades, (see retail price chart 1896-1939, at bottom of page 109). Sign designers graduated from blue and white to include yellow, modifying the sloping lettering to a curve. Then, to accommodate the advertising gimmick of offering £1,000 reward to anyone discovering impurities, the signs with soap packets, and the Sunlight boys were introduced.

All the signs displayed here and the projecting 'flag' were introduced before WWI. The packet at an angle with soap bars slipping out, dates from c.1935. The Indian and South African signs are post-WWII.

Brewery trade

Breweries favoured two strong images; the drinking man and the centralised glass, bottle or label, surrounded by text. Some of these are very similar because they were based on stock images prepared by sign manufacturers. Since most beer was brewed and distributed fairly locally, a neighbouring brewer using an advertising image identical but for the textual content, presented no threat. However, the image of the drinking man was sometimes a trade mark, official or casual, of particular breweries, so investment in making this character distinguishable and different from those of other breweries, became an important issue. Nowhere is this more evident than in the Guinness posters of the mid-1930s to mid-1950s, featuring a zoo-keeper, zoo animals and a few other readily recognisable types, designed by John M Gilroy. Sadly none of these was interpreted in enamel, although several of them have been offered to the public in recent years by the 'repro' trade. The image of the Guinness glass may also be by Gilroy, being executed in his crisp, incisive style.

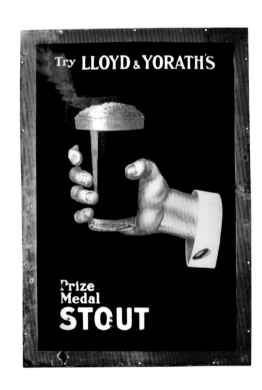

"A.K" Gold Medal Paris 1889
HOLE'S FAMILY ALES
NEWARK on TRENT

MAGNET
ALES

ESTAB^D 1767
OAKHILL ALES & BEERS IN BOTTLE

Established 1780
TRADE MARK
STONE ALE

Jubilee suits me

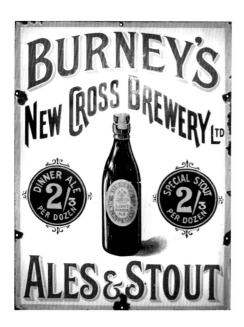

BURNEY'S New Cross Brewery LTD
DINNER ALE 2/3 PER DOZEN
SPECIAL STOUT 2/3 PER DOZEN
ALES & STOUT

ROBERTSON'S "YELLOW LABEL" SPECIAL SCOTCH WHISKY.
JOHN ROBERTSON & SON L^TD DISTILLERS, DUNDEE.

GRANT'S
"STAND FAST"
SCOTCH WHISKY

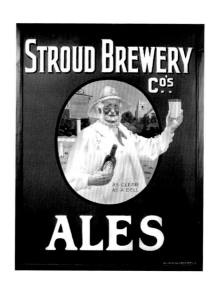

STROUD BREWERY C^OS
AS CLEAR AS A BELL
ALES

INSIST ON
MITCHELL'S XXX BOGIE
ORIGINAL AND BEST

"OLD BUSHMILLS" PURE MALT WHISKEY
Established 1784
DISTILLERY, BUSHMILLS

BEST FOR HEALTH
IRVINE'S
GOLD MEDAL
PARIS 1900   LONDON 1873
PURE AUSTRALIAN WINES
RED & WHITE BURGUNDIES

"KENT'S BEST"
GEORGE BEER AND RIGDEN'S ALES & STOUT
In Bottle & Crates

LENEYS WATERINGBURY
BREW FROM ENGLISH HOPS ONLY

1

2

3

4

5

6

7

8

9

10

11

12

13

15

16

17

18

Enamels from around the world, including Argentina (3/6/7/11/14), Belgium (1), Britain (2/4/5/9/12/16/17/19), Germany (20), China (5/13), Australia (15), Denmark (8), India (18), North Africa (10).

The motif of sunrise as a 'fan' of sunbeams has associations with Art Deco design. But this is occasionally misleading. The Hereford Brewery Golden Sunlight pale ale sign (16) predates the Art Deco period, whereas the Fisk tyre sign, (page 91) and Sternol oil, (page 21) are from the 1920s and 1930s.

Multi-lingual text on signs is unusual in Western advertising, but is a factor that eastern designers have had to contend with for decades. In oriental ports, especially those around the Pacific Rim countries where the population may embrace a dozen different nationalities, cultures, or religions, the 'levelling' factor of commerce has to cater to all. Akbar Shar cigarettes, page 119, Bokser Port, page 115, (13) and Brand's Essence of Chicken, page 165, are just three examples.

14

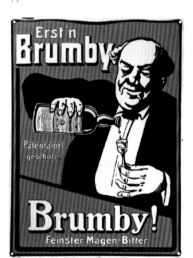

19

20

Tobacco trade

Tobacco product manufacturers, having flirted with elaborate pictorial images around 1900 (see examples on pages 116 to 119), soon settled on the central, tilted packet, as standard. There were some subtle variants , such as exposed filter tips, or 'fanned' cigarettes projecting from the pack. European, South African, North American and Indian designers had more fun with tobacco imagery.

OGDEN'S
COOLIE
CUT PLUG

 St.JULIEN
TOBACCO & CIGARETTES

TURMAC
CIGARETTES

PLAYER'S

PLAYERS NAVY CUT CIGARETTES

NAVY CUT
CIGARETTES

"A Cigarette for every occasion"
Smoke
CHING & C⁰'s
NAVY CUT
CIGARETTES

TABACS
LE DRAGON

FOURNIER-DELCROIX
BLANDAIN

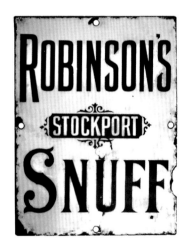

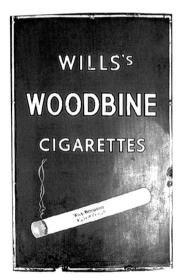

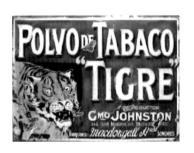

119

Removals and storage

The most celebrated removals sign is for Fraser's of Ipswich. It typifies the product-specific design for this particular trade, having the name of the company written in bold, ornate, free-flowing, fairground-style lettering, on the upper edge of a coloured frame, surrounding a white cartouche on which a steam traction engine and wagon is depicted. This formula was constantly used for removals companies throughout Britain, but does not seem to have caught on in other countries. This may reflect the relatively late onset of enamel sign production elsewhere, at which time motor vehicles would have been the norm. One notable example of a removal sign that does not conform to this pattern is Robsons of Newcastle, where a couple parade before their new home, while the Robsons horse-drawn van is seen to the side, drawn in steep perspective.

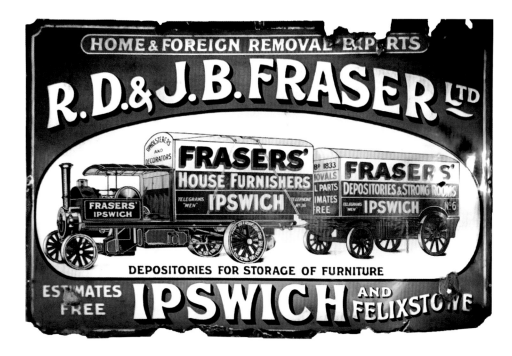

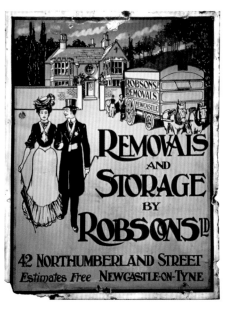

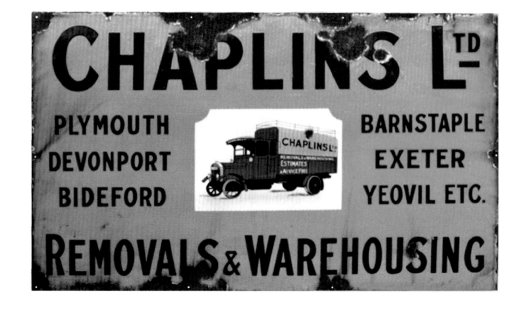

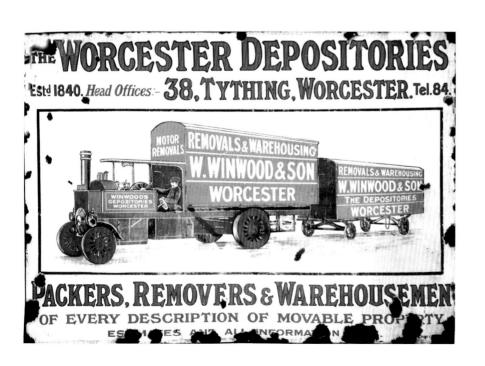

Motoring

For much of the 20th century petrol pumps sported internally lit translucent white globes, bearing company logos. In an attempt to bring some cohesion to garage forecourt advertising displays, many enamel signs featured similar globes, while those that did not, made reference in their text to pumps or other technical petrol specific references. The BP Winner sign has subtle variations in content and execution to the one illustrated in *More Street Jewellery*, implying that the image was a 'winner' in its day, being in demand enough for the sign to be re-drawn on at least two occasions.

It was most unusual to have 'sponsored' road signs, and apparently unpopular, to judge by the vandalism that this Daimler sign attracted. The restorer has achieved a convincing repair.

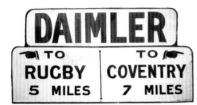

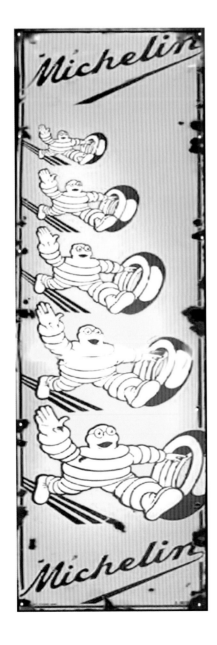

I.M.T
SERVICE

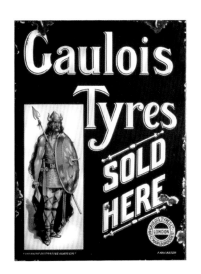

Gaulois Tyres SOLD HERE

MUSGO GASO LINE MICHIGAN'S MILE MAKER

SHELL MOTOR OIL

BATES DUNLOP

STERNOL OILS & GREASES

HUTCHINSON TYRES
THE TYRE WITH NINE LIVES
FOR
CYCLES. MOTOR CYCLES & CARS

AEROSHELL LUBRICATING OIL STOCKED HERE

SHELL MOTOR OILS

Tea

Recurrent symbols on tea signs are the tea leaf, the teacup and the teapot. Other product-specific images or associative motifs less commonly used but still very much in the same genre are the tea picker and the Indian elephant. A recurrent textual theme on tea signs, more commonly found than on adverts for other similar products, are claims of cheapness and economy. The 'Lyons' tea sold here' sign surmounted by the location 'Braintree', has a dual purpose of advertising and directional / location signage similar in rarity to the Daimler shown earlier. The famous Nectar tea teacup, of which hundreds where found hidden in a warehouse in the 1980s, comes in two sizes and three colours (white, green or pink backgrounds). A version of the Brooke, Bonds' 'small spoonful' sign can be seen on a shelf of the Falkirk stencil storage room, (page 51).

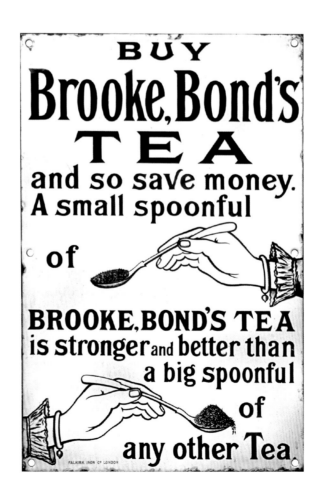

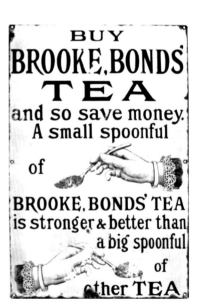

Shops and shopping

Using the subject to advantage: the what and where of street jewellery

For those well off enough to afford it, like the well-to-do mothers and children seen riding or walking on these Cadbury's and Bovril signs, going shopping has been retail therapy for centuries. This was never more so than during the Edwardian era, when so many 'modern' facilities and conveniences historically converged. With the arrival of cheap public transport to augment private vehicles, travelling in and around towns on well maintained metalled roads, lined by paved pedestrian paths, rendered a clean, convenient and safe environment in which to shop. The shop windows, traditionally composed of many small panes separated by wooden frames, became large plate glass showcases, richly framed, carved, painted and inscribed with flourishing calligraphy across the whole frontage. Not only were the wares for sale displayed in the windows, but also elaborate window dressing props such as presentation boxes with richly printed labels, giant size dummy copies of packaging, mirrors with gilded lettering proclaiming products' merits, show-cards, posters and, of course, enamel signs. The signs could be utilised anywhere in the shop environment, indoors and out, and despite their weight and rigidity were effectively the most 'flexible' advertising tool available to the shopkeeper.

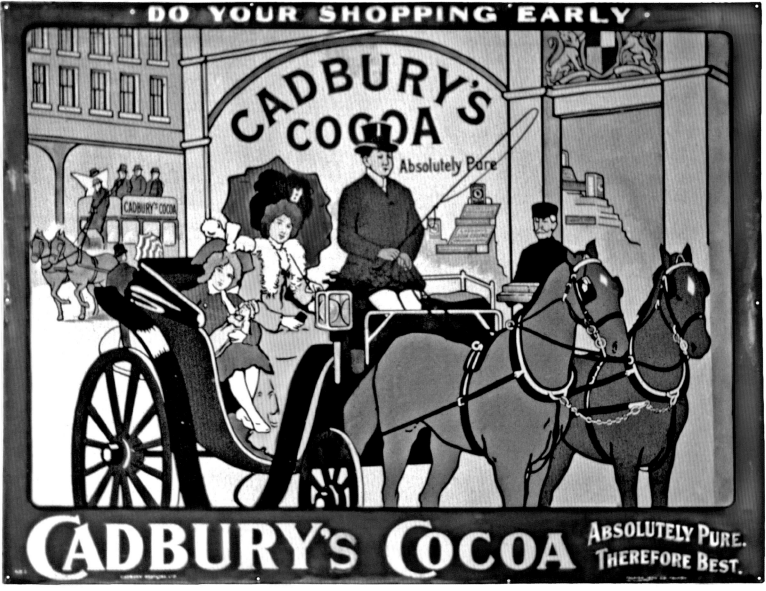

Going shopping sometimes meant an extensive stay in the shop, waiting for products such as butter and sugar to be weighed out and wrapped, bacon sliced, coffee ground, or tea blended. While waiting, customers were provided with seating, courtesy of proprietary soap companies, including Gossage's, Watson's, (page 132), Venus, and in Walter Willson's stores by their own in-house customised chairs. Each stout wooden chair had an enamelled iron sign forming the back plate, some with adverts just on the front, others being double sided. Some companies like Hudson's, and Palethorpe's got their name seen on other shop fittings, such as finger plates, scales, dog-drinking bowls, food platters – *Hunter's Handy Hams* (page 146) – and trays. However, most enamels were two-dimensional and mounted out-of-doors.

In Britain's booming industrial towns and cities, over the course of time, more specialist outlets joined the 'general dealer' type of corner shop, to serve the busy, thriving, populous communities that surrounded factories. Many of the signs illustrated in this section would have been attached to specialist shops selling meat, bread, musical instruments, haberdashery, tobacco, and so on.

Locations for mounting signs could be shops' gable ends, above and below the fascia, on the entrance portico wall, projecting into the street, suspended from metal brackets or chains, on 'A' frames (put outside the shop daily), or on walls and counters within the shop. Quite often, more than one of the same sign would be placed side by side. For the advertiser this had the double benefit of hammering home the message and of keeping the signs of competing businesses at bay! Keeping the opposition off the wall space was a successful tactic, but an additional benefit was the psychological power of repetition; the more often the advertising message was seen and read by the public the more like a shopping 'mantra' it became. Signs on the shop walls could have the power to suggest to the customer about to enter the shop that they should not just read out 'cocoa' from their shopping list, but should ask specifically for Epps's, or Rowntree's or van Houten's. This choice was predicated not only by the efficacy and quality of the advertising, but also by the prominence of its positioning. Eventually, the public automatically used associated advertising slogans when requesting products. Dodd's shop, (page 130), has many examples in enamel, and other media, of adverts with strong slogans. One catch phrase that was so often voiced that it became irritating, attracting satirical comment in *Punch* and elsewhere, was the 'Pear's' response to the daily greeting, *viz*: Person A: '*Good morning!*' Irritating Person B: '*Good morning, have you used Pears' today?*' Television advertising continued the tradition and continues to have a similar effect on contemporary consumers. I recall from my childhood viewing, '*You'll wonder where the yellow went when you clean your teeth with Pepsodent*' (coined by PB Jones for Foote, Cone & Belding in 1956).

Today, toothpaste, along with any other product, can be purchased under the same roof, in a supermarket. Before the 1960s however, the high street was lined with dozens of different specialist shops to an extent hard to imagine by those too young to have experienced them at first hand. The following section recalls those shops and illustrates some of the street jewellery that decorated them.

Tomorrow's antiques on her doorstep

This shopkeeper, having ventured forth from the cosy security of her shop, is standing in the doorway somewhat apprehensively, yet in a typically proprietorial pose. She is surrounded by dozens of signs, most of which are collectable 'classics' nowadays. Close equivalents to some of them are reproduced on this page.

To her and to her customers, this wealth of advertising in enamel, paper, timber and tin was so familiar as to be only subliminally perceived, and certainly not regarded as 'tomorrow's antiques'. The psychological selling power, however, was well recognised by marketers. The wall space taken by each sign was rented from the shopkeeper, thus we can tell from this photograph (and many similar period photographs), that manufacturers thought it worthwhile paying for several identical signs to be mounted on the same site.

A chair like the one below might have been inside the shop, allowing customers to take the weight off their feet while awaiting completion of their orders.

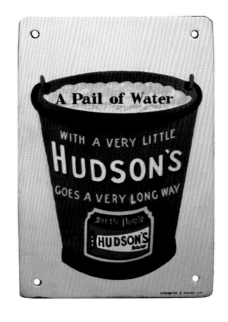

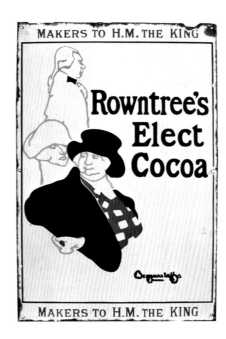

Hardware store:

Typical stock/services included: Household wares, paint, fuel oils, lighting requisites, tools, gadgets, and building materials.

As with many products, hardware, once the stock in trade of high street shops, is now sold from warehouses on retail estates. When shops were within walking distance of urban housing, one of the charming advertising gimmicks that supported this routine was the enamel sign backed chair, for the repose of footsore shoppers. Walter Willson's even had the greeting '*A seat, madam?*' displayed on the back of their chairs. Shopping trips could double as opportunities to exercise dogs, so thoughtful traders provided bowls of water, incidentally advertising Hudson's soap – '*Drink, puppy, drink*', (page 48), Spratt's or Osoko dog biscuits.

As well as building materials, tools, pots and pans, household soap and pet food, hardware shops supplied lighting paraphernalia, such as candles, gas mantles, lamp oil, oil lamps and light bulbs. The stink of burning lamp oil is something that modern house-owners are spared. Shopkeepers selling domestic fuel were often referred to as 'oilmen'. It may be that the fuel oil manufacturers hoped to suggest subliminally that their particular brands would smell fragrant, as suggested by such trade names as White Rose (a rose by any other name!) and White Hyacinth. Materials for the weekly chores, including starch washing soap, were stocked by hardware shops. The traditional day for washing was Monday. On 'washday Monday' clothes were boiled in a 'copper', and 'the wash' was agitated frequently

under hot soapy water with a poss-stick. Wringing out water was achieved with a mangle – turned by hand electric mangles became available (page 133). Additives to the water such as blue bags and borax during washing, improved the final appearance of the fabrics, or protected them, prolonging their useful life. Reckitt's Bag Blue (page 101 and 134) and Borax crystal were two popular additives. After rinsing, those items requiring starch, such as Reckitt's Robin starch (page 134) would be separated, starched and re-wrung. Some laundries offered communal mangling services. Wrung-out washing was taken in a basket, as depicted on several Robin starch signs, and the Puritan 'pure as the breeze' sign (page 135), to a drying ground, over a lawn or in the back lane and pegged on a washing line. 'Good drying weather' was sunny with a light breeze as depicted on Puritan Soap (page 135). Taking in the washing was an art in itself, as careful folding made ironing easier. Stretching linen was managed most easily by two people, but is seen being accomplished using a chin as a 'third hand' in the Colman's starch advertisement (page 134). One of the endearing qualities of Monkey brand soap was the monkey (sometimes rigged out in evening wear), uttering the advertising claim that it '*Won't wash clothes*'! Many other firms like Read's Donkey brand, Bond's and Old Dutch (page 134), made general-purpose soap. Pest controls such as fly killer and rat poison often contained toxins that are now banned.

Nowadays, whereas nearly all baskets, buckets and other containers are manufactured in plastic, there was once a selection of timber, wickerwork, galvanized zinc, ceramic and enamelled iron artefacts to choose from.

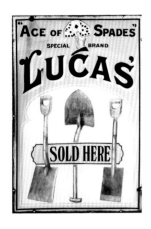

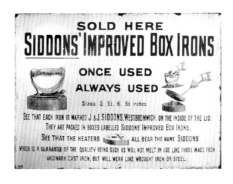

Going, going, gone . . .

Closing down early in this century, Edinburgh's famed string and brush shop, was one of the last survivors of the specialist hardware store.

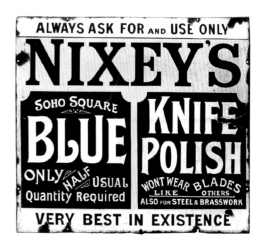

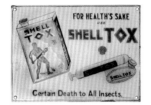

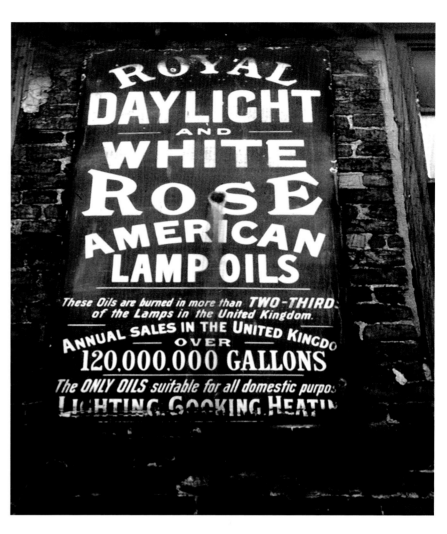

Garage:

Typical stock/services included: Motorcars, motorcycles and automobile products such as petrol, plugs and tyres.

Enamels were designed to promote all the products and services associated with transport, (see also section *Transport*). This section shows some of the products and services available to the shopper using their car. Almost every product associated with the automobile, from tyres to insurance was eventually the subject of enamel advertising imagery. Shell was particularly assiduous in promoting its various oil-based products with enamel signs. The changing face of the famous Shell scallop logo, can be traced in enamel through subtly shifting variations for almost the whole of the 20th century.

Motoring quickly became the passion of wealthy Edwardians, forcing blacksmiths' shops to double as, and eventually convert to, garages with forecourt pumps.

Urban Telegraph

These curved signs were designed to conform to the circumference of telegraph poles, to which they were fixed, their rental revenue presumably going to the Post Office.

MEMBER OF THE NATIONAL MASTER FARRIERS ASSOCIATION

REGISTERED TRADE MARK

CLEVELAND DISCOL

ALCOHOL FOR ENGINE POWER

Bedford TRUCKS

8-CWT TO 3-TON

CENTRAL MOTOR GARAGE

BOWER ROAD

HARROGATE

(Near N.E.R. Goods Yard)

REPAIRS. PETROL

INSPECTION PITS

TYRES

ACCESSORIES ETC.

Accommodation for 100 Cars

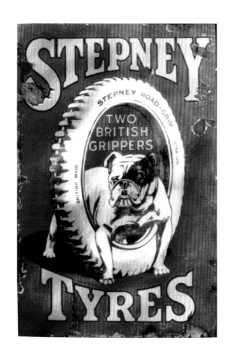

STEPNEY

STEPNEY ROAD-GRIP

TWO BRITISH GRIPPERS

TYRES

ELECTRIC PUMP

DOMINION Guaranteed

AC

AC

AC SPARK PLUG

DURANT

SALES - SERVICE

Mobiloil

REG'D TRADE MARK

OPEN FOR FINA PETROL

CONOCO GASOLINE

REG U.S PAT OFF

BETTER BUY REGENT

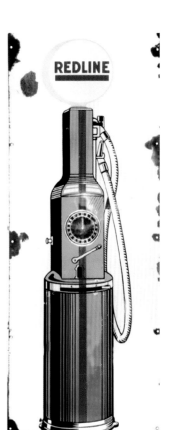

REDLINE

DAGENITE BATTERIES FOR CARS-RADIO-AIRCRAFT

LUBRICATION COMPLETE SPECIALI SERV

As Recommended By The Motor Car Manufacturers

NORTH BRITISH RAPSON

THE WORLD'S LONGEST MILEAGE TYRES

CASTLE Rd SOUTHSEA

PARKER THOMAS

AND COMPANY

FOR YOUR

BAGLA BROS Transports

HEAD OFFICE 149. HARRISON ROAD.

GARAGE & WORKSHOPS

TRANSPORTATION AT LOWE RATE IN CALCUTTA

Grocery, General dealer,
Corner shop, Off license, Pub:

Typical stock/services included: Pre-packaged convenience food, alcohol, tobacco products, household requisites and matches.

The birth of the enamel sign coincided with the birth of the great expansion of pre-packaged foods that by the 1880s had become well established. Earlier in the century, biscuits and branded chocolate, needing only wrappers to make them saleable, were among the first food items to be mass produced in regional factories (eg. Huntley & Palmer's), then transported round the country, but other products needing more sophisticated packaging followed suit. The Quaker Oats brand is reckoned to be one of the very first staple goods to be branded, packed and marketed in the modern way. Soon, with the invention of canning, foods such as salmon, sweet corn and peaches were being canned near their point of production, then transported all over the world. Products as diverse as fish-paste and tooth powder were marketed in sealed ceramic pots, while other goods, including fruit, jam, pickles and sauces, were sold in hermetically sealed glass bottles and jars. Heinz was, of course, the most celebrated and longest lived brand for the latter delicacies. Evidently pre-packaged comestibles warranted costly advertising as no fresh 'fruit & veg' signs exist, except for two promoting Fyffes bananas,

(pages 140 and 222). Some grocery stores, as well as some pubs, doubled as off-licences. In these were sold a variety of bottled beers, wines, champagnes, spirits and 'tonic' drinks*, many of which were advertised by enamel signs, particularly at railway stations. Many general stores, as well as specialist sweet shops, had Fry's, Rowntree's or Cadbury's enamelled copper letters stuck to their windows, because they traded in the popular cocoa powders manufactured by those firms.

In smaller village communities, still the case in rural Eire, pubs doubled as general stores. As a theme, 'alcoholic beverages' yields one of the highest numbers and imaginative variety of enamel signs, comparable in quantity to tobacco and newspapers. The brewing and advertising industries stretched the imaginations of the world's most creative commercial artists. From Argentina to Australia the competition to devise yet more memorable trademarks generated every eye-catching image, from red zebras to tipsy kangaroos. In the final analysis, pictorial representations of the bottles themselves are perhaps the most successful.

* Wincarnis, Wine o' Bos and Bovril wine were all meat extract 'health' beverages, sold at grocery stores and as 'pick-me-ups' at chemists.

NESTLÉ'S SWISS MILK
The Richest in Cream

JAMS AND WIGAN WORKS MAWDSLEY'S MARMALADE

MILKMAID BRAND
STERILIZED NATURAL MILK

Strongest and Best — Health
OVER 220 GOLD
J.S.FRY & SONS COCOA MAKERS BRISTOL & LONDON
Fry's Pure Concentrated Cocoa
MEDALS AND DIPLOMAS
Strongest and Best

le potage de poule naturel
LEMCO Chicken Soup
WITH FINE & DELICIOUS NOODLES
COOKS IN 4 MINUTES
PRODUIT LIEBIG

Tip Top
TOP
Fische

Beach's Jams
and a Wonderful Lemon Curd.

THE KYDD'S JAMS AND MARMALADE BEST

Die vortrefflichen Konservengläser Marke
REX
Anerkannte Verkaufsstelle

Little Miss Vi's BIG CUP
The Food Beverage of the People
Vi-Cocoa
MADE IN DELECTALAND WATFORD

FARMERS BEST
CAREY-IZED SALT
CAREY-IZED SALT
YOUR DEALER HAS IT

SAY'S COCOA

VIKING THE PERFECT UNSWEETENED MILK

TWO OF HEINZ 57

USE WHITE-COTTELL'S PURE MALT VINEGAR
PERFECT FOR PICKLING
BEST AROMA BEST FLAVOUR

WINES AND SPIRITS
THE BEST QUALITY ONLY
John Shaw
MIDLAND ST HULL
NEAR STATION ENTRANCE ANLABY Rd.

Vera
DRUŽSTEVNÍ POLÉVKOVÉ KOŘENÍ
VDP
VELKONÁKUPNÍ SPOLEČNOST DRUŽSTEV PRAHA

OETKER'S
MARMELADEN
MARKE DOMPFAFF

To Be Sure Sailors Eat
QUAKER
In Packets Only
ROLLED WHITE OATS
QUAKER OATS

Beefex
FOR HEALTH

Keen's D.S.F. Mustard
150 YEARS REPUTATION

LA POULE AU POT
LA POULE AU POT
LE CONSOMMÉ PARFAIT
EN VENTE ICI

Yorkshire Relish
is rich and thin — that's why it goes so far.

BOURNVILLE COCOA
BY TEST, THE BEST.

Timothy White's Lemon Crystals
THE IDEAL THIRST QUENCHER.

SILVER SHRED
ROBERTSON'S Lemon Marmalade

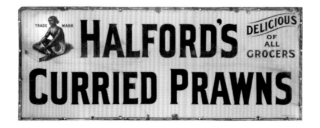

TRADE MARK
HALFORD'S CURRIED PRAWNS
DELICIOUS OF ALL GROCERS

WE SELL OX-HEART BRAND PEANUT BUTTER

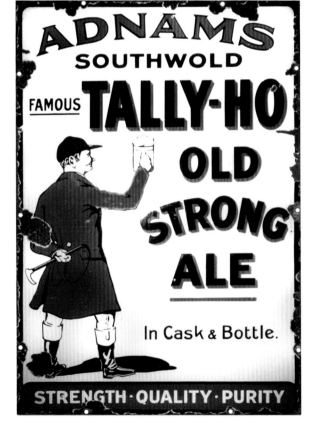

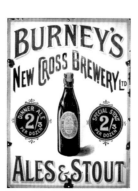

Restaurant, Café, Teashop, Bakery, Hotel:

Typical stock/services included: Refreshments, accommodation, catering, and bakery goods.

Only a few cafés and restaurants could justify the expense of dedicated enamel signs. Some cafés, such as Pumphrey's of the Cloth Market Newcastle, did so because they also retailed tea and coffee, probably regarding a dual purpose advert as potentially profitable. A curious element to the Pumphrey's sign (page 144) is the grid of bamboo canes dividing up the text. The sign's designer evidently wished to reflect Pumphrey's house style which was Chinoiserie – mainly manifested in the willow-pattern ceramics displayed throughout the premises. Most British coffee signs, exemplified by Patterson's Camp Coffee, advertised liquid coffee essence.

In Europe, signs issued by the great coffee merchants Van Houten's and their lesser rivals advertised beans or fresh ground coffee, while in Britain, tea advertising accounted for by far the greatest number of beverage-related enamels, followed by cocoa.

Some British bakers, including Huntley & Palmer's, Lyons, Kunzle and Belvoir, advertised cakes and biscuits on enamel signs. In Britain, Europe and the USA, enamels advertising bread were numerous, as were adverts for flour and baking powder. There were even a few enamel signs advertising yeast.

Railway stations and other transport terminals were the natural environment for hotel enamels such as Higginbottom's, and firms including cafés, such as The Abbey Café, used curved signs that conformed to the surface of telegraph poles, on which they were displayed, along streets adjacent to the premises. John Knight's frying oil is the only enamel evidence of the ubiquitous British fish and chip shop.

MAGIC YEAST MAKES GOOD BREAD

GOODWIN'S EXTRA SELF RAISING FLOUR — THE "BABY" BAG

WE SELL Lyons 2d FRUIT PIES MANY VARIETIES

BE SURE YOU GET THE ROYAL DIADEM HIGH DOUBLE GRADE EXTRA SELF RAISING FLOUR — ASK FOR IT.

THE BEST FISH FRIED IN THE BEST OIL WE USE JOHN KNIGHT'S FRYING OIL ONLY.

Hansa BÄCKEREI

LYONS CAKES

MAGIC YEAST MAKES GOOD BREAD

Bake at home with Brown & Polsons Raising Powder PAISLEY FLOUR Even Beginners Get Good Results

NO BETTER FOOD — FRY'S PURE CONCENTRATED COCOA — FRY'S HIGH CLASS CHOCOLATE — 300 Gold Medals & Diplomas.

Shield of Virtue

A few British enamels have blistered shapes manufactured into their construction. McNiven and Cameron produced a couple in the form of pen nibs, and several other companies, including Singer sewing machines, Fry's cocoa and chocolate and Kennedy's bread, issued signs with blisters in the form of shields. The shield has been an icon for purity and security in Europe since the Middle Ages. The various heraldic crests indicating royal appointment similarly inspire confidence. The Fry's double shamrock blistered sign was designed specifically for the Irish market, as was the Rowntree's chocolate sign with an Irish harp substituted for the British royal coat of arms. Various Cadbury, Fry and Rowntree signs have green backgrounds, said to have had appeal for the Irish market.

RELIABLE RALEIGH Cycles RIGID RAPID — WALTER WILLSON'S Smiling Service Shops — Ford FORD CARS TRUCKS — SUNDAY TIMES PRICE ONE PENNY — SEWING SINGER MACHINES

THE SALVATION ARMY — BP — "Meadowsweet Butter" — BOARD of AGRICULTURE AND FISHERIES. LIGHT HORSE BREEDING KING'S PREMIUM LONDON 1918 — NEW ERA LAUNDRY ART DYERS & DRY CLEANERS

THE WAVERLEY PICKWICK & OWL PENS ARE THE BEST PENS INVENTED — FINEST QUALITY MADE KENNEDY'S BREAD DUBLIN

BY APPOINTMENT TO H.M. THE KING MUMBY'S DRY Ginger Ale

ROWNTREE'S CHOCOLATES

ROWNTREE'S CHOCOLATES AND PASTILLES

"NO BETTER FOOD" FRY'S CHOCOLATE FRY'S COCOA 300 Gold Medals & Diplomas.

WAVERLEY THE WAVERLEY PEN PEN IS A TREASURE MACNIVEN & CAMERON EDINBURGH

EXTRA FANCY QUALITY CHIEF FLOUR AMERICAN MAID FLOUR MILLS U.S.A.

ASK FOR "DCL" YEAST SOLE MANUFACTURERS. THE DISTILLERS COMPANY LD EDINBURGH.

SPECIAL AGENT FOR Kunzle CAKES MADE WITH PURE DAIRY BUTTER & EGGS ALL CAKES ARE FRESH

FINN'S STORES & CAFÉ **CANTERBURY.**
BEST GOODS · LARGEST VARIETY · LOWEST PRICES
IN ALL DEPARTMENTS. FREE DELIVERY
ILLUSTRATED CATALOGUE & TERMS on APPLICATION

HIGGINBOTTOM'S

HOTELS (FAMILY & COMMERCIAL)	RESTAURANTS
PLOUGH HOTEL ALNWICK	"SAVOY" DEAN ST. NEWCASTLE
NORTHUMBERLAND ARMS NEW QUAY, NORTH SHIELDS	POST OFFICE RESTAURANT ST. NICHOLAS SQR. NEWCASTLE
IMPERIAL HOTEL STANLEY, Co. DURHAM.	"RENDEZVOUS" 9, PILGRIM ST. NEWCASTLE

FOR **COMFORT & CUISINE**

WINE **GORDON'S** BAR

T. PUMPHREY & SONS CELEBRATED **COFFEE** SERVED HERE As at Cloth Market Buildings NEWCASTLE on TYNE. The Very Finest Quality Obtainable

You save 4ᴰ a 1b. **Brooke Bond Dividend Tea**

Visit the BON MARCHÉ LUNCHEON AND TEA ROOMS Finest in the City

MORNING COFFEE LUNCHEONS TEAS PHONE 521. **ABBEY CAFE** I. G. SHELTON ABBEY Rd. HOME MADE CAKES SCONES ETC.

TOWER TEA SOLD HERE

HOTEL FOR **GENTLEMEN** BREAKFASTS, DINNERS & TEAS ENTRANCE ROUND CORNER Propr. T. OLIVER.

TRAGT EFTER MIN **KAFFE**

UNEQUALLED FOR FLAVOUR & STRENGTH **JOKO** ¼ lb. NETT PURE CEYLON TEA ¼ lb. NETT GLENTON MITCHELL 231 MAIN STREET JOHANNESBURG AND AT

SIMBA CHAI Kenya Grown Tea Sole Distributors Brooke Bond East Africa Ltd. Kericho

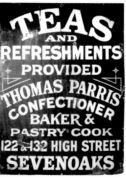

TEAS AND **REFRESHMENTS** PROVIDED THOMAS PARRIS CONFECTIONER BAKER & PASTRY COOK 122 & 132 HIGH STREET **SEVENOAKS**

CIKORKA HRADECKÁ SE ZNAČKOU »TŘI DĚCHA«

DANISH CONDENSED MILK DANCOW DANISH DAIRIES MILK EXPORT COPENHAGEN · DENMARK

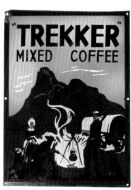

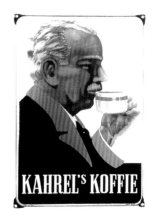

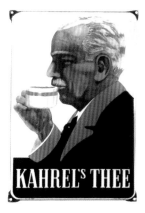

Butcher, Dairy, Fishmonger:

Typical stock/services included: Fresh and cooked meats, sausages, milk, cream, margarine, butter, and fish.

With the exception of the national campaigns promoting Palethorpe's and Walls' sausages and pies, most butchery enamel signs were confined to local suppliers, like Davy's of Sheffield, who issued three remarkable enamels, one illustrated with a pig in a field, one advertising polony and the other brawn. A sign for the Welsh butcher Hetherington's, uses the once widespread custom familiar to butchery window displays. The convention was for small plaster or composition models of pigs, cattle or sheep, to be placed among cuts of meat. The enamel imitation of this gruesome practice has Hetherington's rearing heifer holding a tray of *à la mode* beef supported on its forelegs.

Signs for dairies and fishmongers are very rare, two notable exceptions being the Belfast fishmonger Sawyers and the dairy chain Danish Dairy Company (rivals to the Maypole dairy chain), whose remarkable sign has an image of a cockerel atop a butter-churning barrel. More common are advertisements for dairy products, particularly margarine, milk and cheese, most of which were sold not only at dairies, but also at corner shops and general grocers.

On yer bike!

It should not be forgotten that until the 1960s much meat, fish, dairy and other produce, was home delivered (or sold from) touring commercial vehicles, horse-drawn wagons giving way to motor vans from c.1910 onwards. For local deliveries butchers and other food retailers, employed boys on bikes, on the frames of which were enamel signs emblazoned with the trader's name (like the Lipton example), or on the baskets of which hung an enamelled price list (like the ice-cream example above).

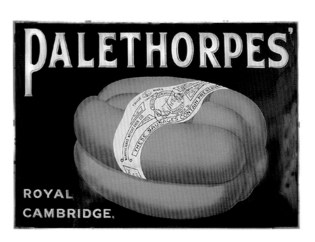

Brug altid
Korsør LØVE-Margarine.

Telephone No 10.   Telegrams. WEBB. WILSON
WEBB & WILSON.
Purveyors OF MEAT.
ICE MERCHANTS. — ARMY CONTRACTORS.
OFFICERS' MESSES SUPPLIED. — MOTOR DELIVERY SERVICE.
11. BRIDGE St. ANDOVER.

AWARD
SPONSORED BY   PROPERTY OF
CALIFORNIA DAIRY INDUSTRIES ASSOCIATION
DAIRY OF MERIT

SVEA-MARGARIN
KALMAR
"Gräddrikast"

LUNHAM'S
FAVOURITE
MILD HAMS
A SPECIALITY
THE CENTRAL PROVISION STORES
3. LAVITT'S QUAY,
CORK.

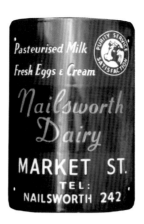

Pasteurised Milk
Fresh Eggs & Cream
Nailsworth
Dairy
MARKET ST.
TEL:
NAILSWORTH 242

USE
Presmilk
6c
IT KEEPS

"DE BOTERMIJN"
MELKVEE SCHILFERS

MARGARINE
Rama
butterfein

Ross's Ideal Milk
"Justice to both"

SAWERS
FOR FISH
HIGH ST
BELFAST

LA VACHE qui RIT

PURE CREAMERY BUTTER
KEVENTER'S
BUTTER
ON SALE HERE

TELEPHONE 75
CANTERBURY
LAMB
DAIRY FED
PORK
ONLY PRIME
ENGLISH MEAT
AT
KEEN CITY PRICES
W. S. HAMLETT
FAMILY BUTCHER
25 BATH HILL, KEYNSHAM.
PERSONAL SUPERVISION.

DELICIOUS IRISH
CREAMERY BUTTER

GRADE
ASK
FOR
METZGER'S
MILK

EAT
COLMAN'S MUSTARD
WITH
OUR PRIME BEEF, MUTTON &c.
AND ENJOY THEM MORE.

BRITISH EXPRESS
DAIRY
CHOICEST   SWEETEST
PUREST   SAFEST
Engine Brand
THE FINEST TABLE BUTTER OF INDIA

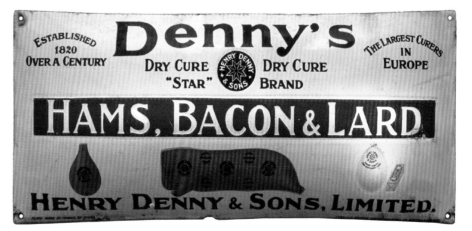

ESTABLISHED
1820
OVER A CENTURY
Denny's
DRY CURE   DRY CURE
"STAR"   BRAND
THE LARGEST CURERS
IN
EUROPE
HAMS, BACON & LARD.
HENRY DENNY & SONS, LIMITED.

LICENSED TO SELL TOBACCO

Tobacconist:

Typical stock/services included: Tobacco products and equipment and matches.

A visit to a tobacconist might involve the purchase of cigars, cigarettes, tobacco, or any of a dozen smoker's requisites. With a tobacco license even a barber could sell tobacco, (page 166). The mid- to late-19th century saw a huge increase in the use of tobacco products around the world. At the turn of the 20th century, the testimony of early newsreels, like those of Mitchell & Kenyon, and informal photographs, show that many men – and increasingly women – smoked in public. The First World War had as one of its dire side effects, a virtual equalisation of smoking between men and women. The medical profession was divided in its opinion as to the health hazards that might be associated with smoking. The public only had access to ambiguous information that failed to curb the steady increase in the popularity of smoking. This would probably have increased irrespective of advertising, as once started, the addictive nature of tobacco kept adherents under its spell. As early as the 1930s, deaths from cancer, notably that of George V, provoked newspaper headlines naming tobacco as a killer. An ironic response to such negative publicity is reflected in enamel advertisements, when Carreras suggest that their cork filter tips would prevent ill effects. The two infamous slogans – *Craven 'A' will not affect your throat',* and *For your throat's sake smoke Craven 'A',* (pages 150-151), appear on stylish Carreras signs during the period.

The tobacco industry was hugely profitable, so despite the generic product having already been 'sold' to the population, individual manufacturers maintained a stream of varied advertising campaigns. These included not only a burgeoning of printed advertising of all types, the introduction of cigarette cards and gift coupons, but also a constantly fresh supply of spectacular enamel advertising signs. This was

in order to encourage the public to keep brand faithful or to switch from a rival company's brand. In and around 1905 a curious banding together of the big British tobacco firms was triggered by a 'raiding party' from the Wild West. USA tobacco magnate James Buchanan (Buck) Duke landed in Liverpool, chequebook in hand, declaring, *'Boys, I've come to buy you out!'* In a nervous rush of proprietorial panic Ogden's, Wills's, Player's, Carreras, plus other smaller British companies, formed the United Tobacco Company in the face of American aggression. After considerable wrangling, a deal was struck that resulted in an Anglo-American consortium. On the lower edge of many tobacco product enamels made in the aftermath of this emergency coalition, can be found printed the legend 'British and American Tobacco Company'.

Before the trade war ended, British firms tried many marketing ploys to keep American tobacco at bay. Price slashing was found not to be enough. Patriotism had to be brought to bear, and a good many advertisements of the time made a direct appeal to the smoking public to buy British. At about the same time a Swedish match company was attempting hostile takeovers of British match companies, who likewise appealed to the British public to support British labour. This aggressive propaganda war which occurred between the Boer War and WWI, urged the British public to keep 'Johnny Foreigner' at bay and must have had a strong psychological effect on the population.

Below: Two views of a bow fronted shop window indicate how large enamelled metal sheets can be curved to fit a contoured wall.

The livery that delivered

Designs for Ogden's signs fall into six main groups. The earliest (Victorian) is a disparate group (Sweet Caporal etc), and has few design characteristics in common. The next group, mainly for Guinea Gold, typically with images of smokers and often with punning slogans, was issued in the early 1900s. Then a white, red and black series, matching similar campaigns by Wills and Player's, filled the post WWI period. The 'look' of the next 'wave', in the 1930s, is given unity by being limited to primary colours – ultramarine background (or occasionally black, as in Impi, Beano and Pigtail), with yellow and red lettering. This was either adopted by, or more likely offered as an incentive to some tobacconists, for their shop nameplates, as in WJ Rugg and A Hughes, Wholesale & Retail Tobacconists. The full range of enamel signs in this blue, red and yellow livery as issued by the Imperial Tobacco Company (Ogden Branch) appears in a rare brochure of March 1938, a photograph on the last page of which shows a frontage flanked with tall narrow signs. The text claims this format 'Helps to keep the shop front tidy, as the wall cannot be used for fly posting'. The number of brands Ogden advertised by these distinctive colourway enamels, was far greater than any other British tobacco manufacturer. St. Bruno and St. Julien were the favourites; others included Robin, Redbreast, Battleaxe Bar, Uncle Toby, Guinea Gold, Juggler, Richmond Gem, Coolie Cut Plug, Walnut Plug and Thunder Clouds. The many signs with tile and brick patterned backgrounds were issued at the same time. We assume that the visually least successful series appeared post WWII, with a yellow background and white-shadowed blue type.

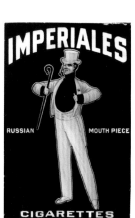

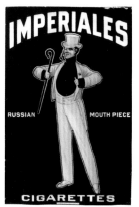

For your throat's sake smoke Craven "A"

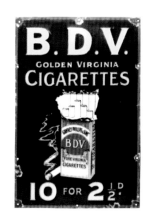

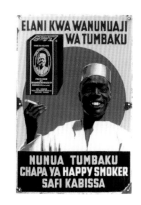

Newsagent, Stationer, Printer:

Typical stock/services included: Daily papers, periodicals, stationery and printing.

In an age when the masses became literate, the demand for stationery items became huge, and the rivalry between manufacturers of pen nibs and ink became fierce. During the late 19th century Birmingham nib manufacturers were producing millions of steel nibs every year. Stephen's 'won the prize' as chief ink and glue monitor! The Edinburgh firm of Macniven & Cameron became a market leader in steel nibs and one of only a few British advertisers to commission enamelled iron signs that had the

iron moulded into blisters in the shape of the product. This process was employed on two pen signs, where the nibs are represented in high relief as bulbous projections rising from the remaining flat surface, (page 143). Macniven & Cameron, Swan and Waterman was one of the first firms to produce fountain pens (perfected by 1883) and then to advertise them on enamels.

Newspapers and journals were heavily advertised on enamel signs. In 1855 the duty on newspapers was abolished and immediately a great expansion occurred in the number of titles published. From then on, throughout the country, nearly every town had at least one local daily or weekly paper. The number of national papers also grew, stimulating the number of enamels promoting papers, as well as increasing growth in secondary advertising campaigns which in turn would be backed up by street advertising.

Although most newspaper enamels had text only designs, like the *West Sussex Gazette*, (page 153 (5), a few were magnificently illustrated including the *Wellington Journal & Shrewsbury News*, *The Sketch* (page 87), *The Passing Show (page 99)*, *John Bull*, *Punch* and *The Field*.

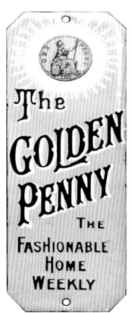

2

5

6

7

8

9

4

His nibs

By the stationer's window (1, far right) is a Stephens' ink thermometer and a Swan double-sided hanging sign for fountain pens, similar to (2) & (3). The newspaper office corner premises (6) is clad with cigarette signs. Clearly this shopkeeper (4) is not a newsagent, nor is his premises a newsagent's shop! Even so, an enamel, similar to (5), for a local paper, is fixed under the window. This would imply that the grocer kept a supply of the papers, or that the premises had changed use.

The Waverley sign (8) is unusual, in that a direct photograph of a 19th-century portrait of Sir Walter Scott has been used to produce the enamelled image by photo-litho half-tone. It may be compared, from the point of view of technical progress, with the similar portrait, (9), using the basic stencilling technique. Mr. Golding (7) has apparently painted out two signs, presumably because he no longer sells the products they advertised.

Sweet shop and Confectioner

Typical stock/services included: Soft drinks, ice cream and sweets.

Down the years tobacconists and newsagents have sold not only tobacco products, but sweets, soft drinks and chocolates. However, for much of the 19th and early 20th centuries, there were many shops specialising only in confectionery. Fry's, Rowntree's and Cadbury's commanded the market in chocolate sales, though many smaller firms held their share of the market.

The sweet shop is now largely a thing of the past. Yet, when such emporia ruled the waking and dreaming hours of the urban child, they were as common as any other specialist shops.

A fashion for stained glass panels in the doors and windows of domestic and business premises is evidenced by a rare Rowntree's chocolates sign (right), that is mocked up to look like a leaded glass panel, doubtless designed to imitate actual leaded glass in a York sweetshop, possibly the factory outlet.

We lament the passing of certain favourite brands of sweet, Fry's Five Boys chocolate the best remembered among them, but there are some, like Rowntree's clear gums, at over a century old (Victoria's royal warrant helps date the sign), that are of great longevity, surviving even half a century beyond the celebrated 1956 TV ad slogan, '*Don't forget the fruit gums, mum!*'

BATEY's
JOHN BULLS
FAVORITE
GINGER BEER

Fry's
CELEBRATED
CHOCOLATE

UNEQUALLED
WE SELL
"VICTORY"
-V-
GUMS
AND
LOZENGES
ALWAYS RELIABLE

Slack & Cox's
GOLD MEDAL
TABLE
WATERS
MANCHESTER

Ringers

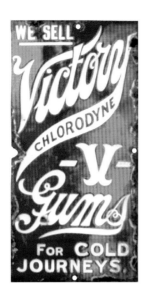

WE SELL
Victory
CHLORODYNE
-V-
Gums
FOR COLD
JOURNEYS

R.WHITE'S
HOUSEHOLD JAR
GINGER BEER   LEMONADE
KAOLA   LIMEADE
GINGER ALE   LEMON SQUASH
SOLD BY GROCERS, CONFECTIONERS, DAIRYMEN, OFF LICENSEES.
DELIVERED FREE

DIXON & SONS
CHEMISTS
HIGH CLASS   ESTABLISHED 1709
MINERAL WATER
MANUFACTURERS
HAYWARDS HEATH & EAST GRINSTEAD

BEVROCK
TABLE WATERS
PURITY GUARANTEED

CORONA
Sparkling Drinks
and Fruit Squashes

Schweppes
SODA WATER. GINGER ALE DRY OR SWEET
TONIC WATER. LIME JUICE.

WE SELL
Victory
-V-
Gums
FOR
COLD
JOURNEYS

R.WHITE's
GINGER BEER
FOR LUNCHEON, DINNER & SUPPER

MONSTERS
1D PINT

BOVRIL
BOVRIL WINE
BOVRIL LOZENGES

1D A GLASS 1D
VANTAS
SPARKLING DRINKS

Drink
TIZER
The Appetizer

AGENCY
Whitman's
SINCE 1842   CHOCOLATES AND CONFECTIONS

WRIGLEY'S   THE FLAVOR
SPEARMINT
PEPSIN GUM   LASTS
TRADE MARK REGISTERED
LOOK FOR THE SPEAR

TOBLER'S
SWISS MILK
CHOCOLATE
A HIGH CLASS PRODUCT
MANUFACTURED AT BERNE (SWITZERLAND)

Harrington's
MINERAL WATERS

Coca-Cola   The Ideal Brain Tonic
TRADEMARK

Finks   The FINEST on the SOUTH COAST
TABLE WATERS AND FRUIT CRUSHES

DELICIOUS & ECONOMICAL
66 Walters' 99
Palm
Toffee
4 OZS 4D
"Worth Double the Price!"

BATEY's
GINGER BEER

ALEXANDERS
PURE TABLE WATERS
SOLD   HERE.

FENN'S
MINERAL WATERS
FARNHAM

DRINK
BATEY's
GINGER BEER
AT MEALS.

CHOCOLATE CREAM

Ice cream parlour

Typical stock/services included: Ice cream, coffee, milkshakes and cakes.

Several waves of Italian immigrants brought with them to the British seaside the glories of the gelataria. It is said they were 'short changed' by unscrupulous shipping companies, who dropped them off in Glasgow, with false assurances that it was New York. Itinerant ice cream vendors with donkey drawn carts, or on bikes, sold scoops of ice cream in glass cups called 'penny licks'. When the ice cream had been licked off, customers returned the cups which were casually rinsed in a bucket of water. This unhygienic practice contributed to the spread of tuberculosis and was banned. Cones, sandwich wafers and waxed card tubs were invented as substitutes and became established as standard.

In the ice cream parlour photograph (below), several Fry's Five Boys showcards are arranged behind the counter and bottles of milkshake flavourings line the upper shelves. Changing times and changing tastes are reflected in the Frozen Yogurt sign, which, dating from the 1980s, must number among the very last commercially commissioned enamel signs to be produced.

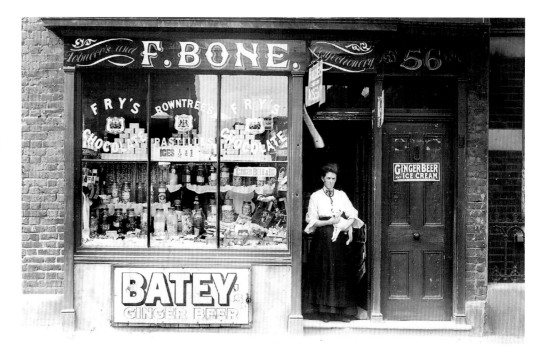

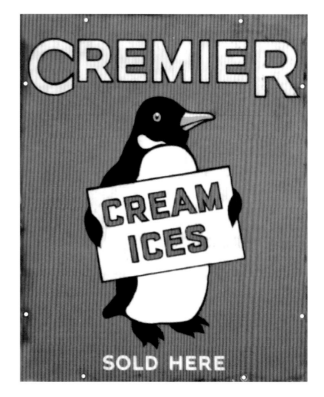

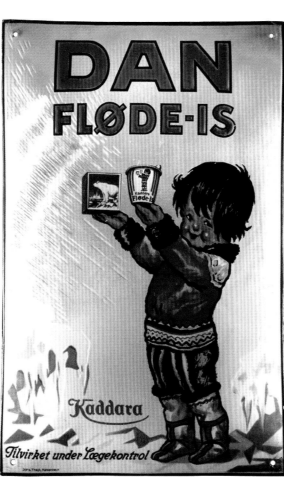

Outfitter, Hatter, Wool shop, Haberdasher, Dry cleaner, Laundry, Cobbler

Typical stock/services included: Haberdashery, clothes, shoes, hats, umbrellas and repairs.

High street and local shopping streets used to have many more clothing shops than one sees today. Gentlemen's and military outfitters, furriers, outfitters specialising in work clothes and school uniforms, ladies boutiques, bespoke tailors and dressmakers, corsetières, milleners, haberdashers, wool shops and shoe shops abounded. Until the 1960s, it was uncommon to see anyone going about bare headed. Then for thirty years hats went out of fashion and most specialist hatters went out of business. The rarely seen bowler hat became a symbol of the city gent, rather than a commonplace business hat. The wearing of 'toppers' is now largely confined to equestrianism, funeral directors, flunkies, ringmasters and wedding guests; straw hats to a few private schools, while trilbies mainly grace the heads of members of the racing fraternity. Recently, however, there has been a resurgence in hat wearing, particularly amongst the young who sport ski balaclavas, down brims, baseball caps and sloppy hoods.

Enamel signs like Ogden's St. Julien '*Officer & gentleman*' can remind us of the ubiquity of hat wearing in former times.

The clothes of the women who adorn many enamel signs are indicative of the prevailing fashion. Walking the streets at the turn of the 20th century, the public could see fashionable reflections of each other captured in the enamelled surfaces of advertisements. We can 'time travel' along the same streets by viewing a display of enamels such as those depicting lace-bonneted housemaids, like Chiver's carpet soap (page 215) and Wood Milne repairs (page 163); fashionable beauties, like the Chlorodont girl (page 212) in fur stole and toque, or stately dames, as in Opel sewing machines (page 211) and Aquascutum (right). By studying such street jewellery 'fashions in aspic' we can imagine strolling with the *beau monde* along a long-gone boulevard.

Outfitters specialising in children's and babies' clothing are now mainly located in department stores rather than in single purpose high street retailing outlets. Such stores stocked items as diverse as prams and nappies as well as clothing.

All the requirements for producing garments knitted at home were available at wool shops, from traditional needles to sewing and knitting machines; from knitting patterns to a staggering array of balls and skeins of wool. These items were always in stock. Balls of wool had factory numbers on them to identify the dye batch, so that extra wool could be ordered without fear of colour mis-matching. Haberdashers also carried items as varied as buttons, hatbands, embroidery silk, elastic and umbrellas, thus providing the requisites for home garment making.

Laundries took in dyeing as well as drapery, clothing and textile cleaning.

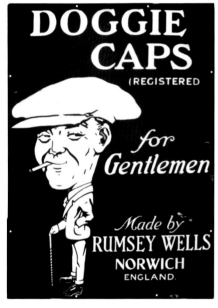
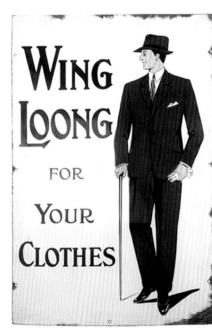
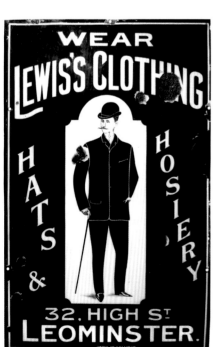

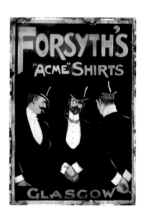

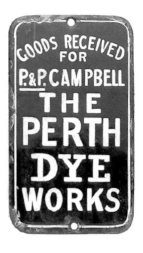

GOODS RECEIVED FOR P.&P.CAMPBELL THE PERTH DYE WORKS

AGENT FOR PULLARS' DYE WORKS PERTH — GOODS Received Here

LES LAINES DU CHAT BOTTÉ LAINES DE SÉCURITÉ

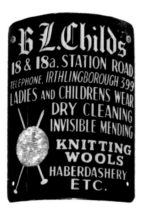

B.L.Childs 18 & 18a. STATION ROAD, TELEPHONE, IRTHLINGBOROUGH 399 LADIES and CHILDRENS WEAR DRY CLEANING INVISIBLE MENDING KNITTING WOOLS HABERDASHERY ETC.

AGENT FOR W.&J. BOWIE DYERS & FRENCH CLEANERS GLASGOW

FOR THE BEST VALUE all BABY & CHILDREN'S WEAR SHOP AT BABYLAND 71 HIGH ST BLAINA

AGENT FOR THE SCOTTISH WATERPROOF CO LTD EDINBURGH ORDERS & REPAIRS RECEIVED HERE

LEYTONSTONE'S OWN BABY STORE BAIRNSFAYRE LTD. 556 HIGH ROAD OPPOSITE THE LEYTONSTONE BOWL PRAMS NURSERY GOODS TOYS

JAEGER purewool WEAR FOR DAY & NIGHT

Schmidt'sche Wolle.

Güter-mann ovo šici hedvábi

Robin Wools are Different

KAWO Korsetter Buste-holdere

Don't Get Wet! MACINTOSHES RAINCOATS OILSKINS UMBRELLAS Stocked in all Prices

"Two Steeples" PURE WOOL UNDERWEAR WILL NOT SHRINK.

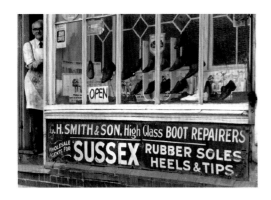

Thrift as a virtue engendered by necessity is an aspect of everyday life well exemplified by enamel adverts for boots, shoes and their repair. Many signs emphasise robust construction more than style or comfort, the exceptions being Jaeger boots & shoes (this page) and Key boots (page 165). The well-known signs for Norfolk boots (page 163) and Oceanic boots & shoes (page 163) still hold their own as powerful, richly coloured and detailed designs compared to the plain, rugged adverts for CC & M Lion and Bull Dog brands (page 163). A feature of several of the boot and shoe adverts is that they advertise locally produced footwear. Kiwi boot polish originated in Australia in 1906. Several polish makers including Cherry Blossom issued shoe-polishing stands clad in enamel signs (below).

Some shoe shine signs

Street corner 'shoe shine boys' used low platforms with a foot rest with which they plied their trade. Boot and shoe polish manufacturers provided these as moveable advertising sites.

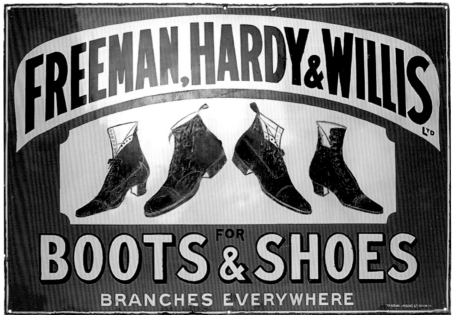

"NUGGET" BOOT POLISH — TIGER BRAND

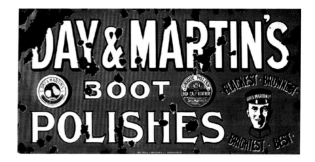

DAY & MARTIN'S BOOT POLISHES — BLACKEST, BROWNEST, BRIGHTEST, BEST

REPAIRS Wood Milne SHOESHINES

I always have a light boot bill because I wear WOOD-MILNE RUBBER HEELS

The BASS SHOE — FOR HARD SERVICE

SUNBEAM BOOT POLISH

AGENT FOR GRIP BRAND BOOTS

KEY BOOTS — MADE IN ENGLAND

STEAD & SIMPSON LTD FOR RELIABLE BOOTS — BRANCHES EVERYWHERE

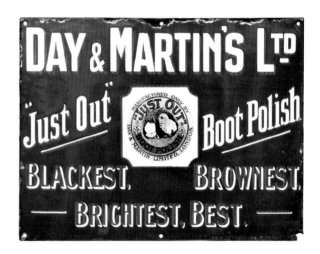

DAY & MARTIN'S LTD — "Just Out" Boot Polish — BLACKEST, BROWNEST, BRIGHTEST, BEST.

WALK-OVER — ONE PRICE 16/6 — AMERICA'S LEADING SHOE — R.K. SMITH, KING'S BUILDINGS ABERDEEN

DUNLOP Boots — AS BRITISH AS the Land!

BUY "Trusty" BRAND BOOTS — "TRUE AS STEEL"

LOTUS SHOES

Schmoll Pasta

DEPÔT FOR "OCEANIC" FOOT-WEAR

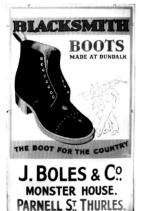

BLACKSMITH BOOTS MADE AT DUNDALK — THE BOOT FOR THE COUNTRY — J. BOLES & CO. MONSTER HOUSE. PARNELL ST. THURLES.

ASK FOR C.C.&M. LION BRAND BOOTS & SHOES

DEPÔT for NORFOLK CHAMPION BOOTS

WEAR ONLY C.C.&M BULL DOG NAILED BOOTS

CASH & CO. THE BEST HOUSE FOR SOLID LEATHER BOOTS. 14. SHEEP MARKET. SPALDING.

Geo. Oliver — THE LARGEST RETAILER IN THE WORLD OF BOOTS & SHOES

Pharmacy, Optician, Dentist, Barber, Surgical supplier:

Typical stock/services included: Medicine, lenses, toiletries, prosthetics and shaving requisites.

Before the advent of the pharmaceutical giants and chain store chemists, local druggists made up pills and potions on prescription for those who could afford the doctor's fee. For the less well off, dozens of proprietary medicines were available for a few pence. Beecham's pills, for instance, though quite expensive at a shilling, were *'worth a guinea a box'* according to the slogan on the box. Many other potions of more or less placebo value, from Flumis flu cure (page 165) to Bunter's Nervine (page 167), tempted the impoverished sick to part with their few coppers in the hope of miraculous cures. Those opposed to advertising in its early days, seized on adverts for quack medicines as examples of why advertising should be curbed. Newspapers that profited from running adverts for dubious treatments claimed that they were not responsible for checking out the propriety of what their advertisers had for sale, suggesting instead that their readers should follow the maxim *caveat emptor*. Chemists who mounted adverts on their shop walls for the likes of Collis Browne's Chlorodine (right), would often offer their poorest customers a generic equivalent of their own concoction at a fraction of the price.

Chemists and pharmacies also sold requisites for hygiene, such as soap, 'pick-me-ups', some of which, like Wincarnis (right), made gloriously extravagant claims for their products, frequently with the alleged backing of an exaggerated number of medical practitioners. Horridly fascinating, but only few in number, are the signs advertising artificial limbs, wigs and false teeth, such as Templar Mallins (page 210).

Opticians and oculists are better represented, and one in particular – AR Baines (page 166), doubled as a surgical appliance maker and offered for sale at his establishment not only spectacles, but also opera glasses, race glasses and cutlery! So far we have found only three enamels advertising perfume (page 165).

1460   KNARESBOROUGH. OLDEST CHEMISTS SHOP IN ENGLAND

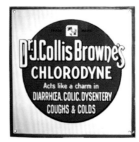

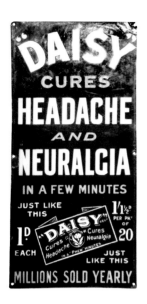

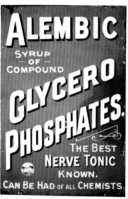

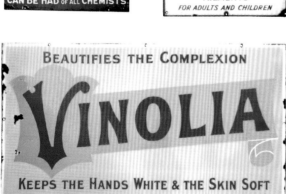

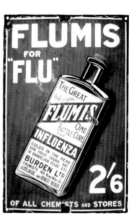

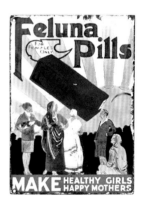

Something for the weekend, Sir?

A small town barber would often augment his income by selling papers, tobacco, sweets, contraceptives and shaving requisites. This barbershop has a huge stripy pole reaching out over the road. I wonder if the barber at the door was aware of the street urchin (far right), as cheeky as the crossing sweeper in Ogden's Guinea Gold 'Beware of Imitations', leaning against a BVD enamel, immediately next to the slogan 'King of smokes'.

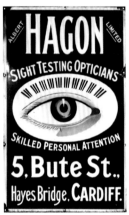

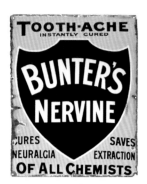

TOOTH-ACHE
INSTANTLY CURED
BUNTER'S
NERVINE
CURES   SAVES
NEURALGIA   EXTRACTION
OF ALL CHEMISTS

PETTIE & COMPANY
548   TRUSSES DUNDEE
ARTIFICIAL LIMBS
SURGICAL APPLIANCES
RUPTURE TRUSSES
ARTIFICIAL EYES
SURGICAL INSTRUMENT MAKERS
TO DUNDEE INFIRMARY
128. NETHERGATE DUNDEE

OUTLASTS 3 Ordinary Brushes

Pro·phy·lac·tic
Derma Grip
TOOTH BRUSH

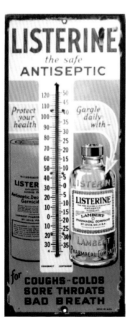

LISTERINE
the safe
ANTISEPTIC

Protect your health   Gargle daily with—

for COUGHS·COLDS
SORE THROATS
BAD BREATH

Odol
The Best for
Mouth and Teeth.

ODOL

Odol

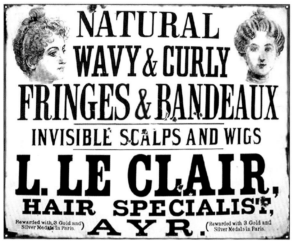

NATURAL
WAVY & CURLY
FRINGES & BANDEAUX
INVISIBLE SCALPS AND WIGS
L. LE CLAIR,
HAIR SPECIALIST,
Rewarded with 3 Gold and   AYR.   (Rewarded with 3 Gold and
Silver Medals in Paris.)   Silver Medals in Paris.

BLUE
GILLETTE
BLADES

"VALET"
Auto-Strop
Safety Razor
STROPS ITSELF.

STOMATOL
Friska, starka,
pärlvita tänder

RAZOR BLADES
DREAD·NOWT
—BRITISH MADE—
2D
TO FIT   TO FIT   TO FIT
EVER READY   GILLETTE   AUTO-STROP
TYPE.   TYPE.   TYPE.
SHAVE SIR?

PEBECO
WEISSE ZÄHNE

KALODONT
beste
Zahn·Crème
Erfrischender
Geschmack

DENTINOL
PASTA PARA LOS DIENTES

MACLEANS PEROXIDE
Tooth Paste
MACLEANS PEROXIDE TOOTH PASTE
makes
teeth WHITER

"GINGE" No 20
LUXUS
Den skarpeste Klinge
er GINGE
faas overalt! 10-15-20-25 ØRE

Chlorodont
Chlorodont

AGENT FOR
THE
FRAM REGD
REAL GERMAN
HOLLOW GROUND
RAZOR
PRICE 4/6 EACH
NEVER REQUIRES
GRINDING

BLUE SEAL
Vaseline
POMADE

BLUE SEAL   Vaseline POMADE
AN EXCELLENT PRESERVATIVE
CHESEBROUGH MFG CO CONS'D
NEW YORK U.S.A.

THE CLEMAK FACE
5/
THE
CLEMAK
Safety Razor

HOME
SAFETY RAZOR

167

Department Store & Co-op:

Typical stock/services included: Household requisites, from furniture to buttons, usually sold by many specialist shops.

The 19th-century saw the development of the shopping mall, one of the first being the Galleria in Milan of 1865. There were up-market department stores like Fenwick, and down-market dime store / cheap chain stores like Woolworth. Few chain stores issued enamel signs, but some lesser-known department stores and large grocers like Walter Willson and Bainbridge in Newcastle, Hill and Sharpe on the Isle of White and the French store Casino,

did so. The British store that eventually opened the most branches, serving a bigger customer base than any other was the Co-operative Wholesale Society. The Co-op, as it became known, was established in Manchester in 1862. By 1900 it had branches in every county, most large cities and many country towns and villages. It used several trade names for its own goods; 'Pelaw', after the town near Gateshead where the polish and shirt factories were located, 'Lutona' after the Luton factory, or 'Wheatsheaf' if made in Manchester. The French Casino chain commissioned its stylish enamel mascot (below) from acclaimed graphic designer Cassandre.

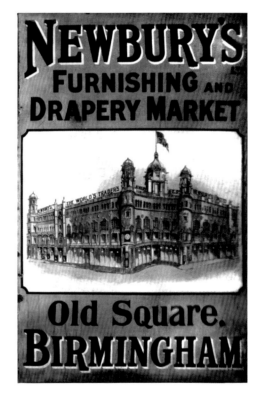

SAMUEL HILL
FURNITURE & CARPETS
REMOVALS AND STORAGE
SAMUEL HILL
DUDLEY & WORDSLEY
HOUSE FURNISHER
ESTIMATES FREE.
DUDLEY AND WORDSLEY.

For CLOUDLIKE
CUSHIONY COMFORT
CHOOSE A
Madad
INNER SPRING
MATTRESS
AT ALL
LEADING STORES

BARKERS
KENSINGTON
HIGH STREET. S.W.
IN THIS DISTRICT
DELIVER FREE

Muebles "El Sol"
FABRICANTES
LUIS TORETTI e Hijo
Casa Argentina Fundada en 1894
CORRIENTES
BUENOS AIRES

R. MADDOX & Co Ltd
SHREWSBURY.
REMOVAL CONTRACTORS
FURNITURE, CARPETS. MODERN DEPOSITORY.
HOUSE AGENTS, UNDERTAKERS.
LADIES MENS & BOYS COMPLETE OUTFITTERS.
GRAMOPHONES, BABY CARRIAGES, SEWING MACHINES.

Quilmes Cristal

ANDRÉS MONTI

HILL'S STORES LIMITED
RYDE I.W.
FOR
STERLING VALUE
IN ALL DEPARTMENTS

BRANDON & SONS,
COMPLETE HOUSE FURNISHERS.
PHONE 10
PHONE 10
REMOVALS
BERKHAMSTED

FURNISH THROUGHOUT WITH
SNOWBALL'S Ltd
GATESHEAD
ILLUSTRATED CATALOGUES FREE
LARGEST STOCK. BEST VALUE
ALL GOODS CARRIAGE PAID

HALL Bros
(F. HALL)
CHINA & GLASS
Riveted
Repaired
Restored
Right
HERE
ENQUIRIES FIRST FLOOR

RING NOW, OR CALL IN FOR
FREE PLANNING AND ESTIMATING
SERVICE
W.A. TAYLOR & SONS
SPECIALIST IN FITTED
CARPETS

MÖBELHAUS
Achille Levy
Oberer
Marktplatz
GEBWEILER
früh. Fabrik
Althofer

CHING-FU
bohnert u. reinigt
Parkett u. Linoleum
CHEMISCHE INDUSTRIE A.-G. ERLANGEN

A.J. SHARPE
COMPLETE HOUSE FURNISHER.
LONDON STORE PRICES
CARRIAGE PAID TO ALL PARTS OF THE ISLAND.
ESTIMATES FREE.
Spring Hill
VENTNOR
Spring Hill

BUDERUS

171

Household suppliers, Removals firms, Auctioneers, Antiques shops, Estate agents, Builders' merchants, Decorators, Utilities, Financial institutions:

Typical stock/services included: Removals, house sales, furniture and requisites, decorating materials and services, gas, electricity and telephone and mortgages.

Removals, house sales

Well into the era of the internal combustion engine, great steam-powered road haulage vehicles, wreathed in palls of smoke and steam, lumbered along the highway delivering heavy goods. At modern steam traction engine rallies the sense-assaulting noise and smell of these mighty vehicles can still be experienced. The weightiness of the process was reflected in the imagery on removals firms' advertising at the turn of the 20th century. Fraser's of Ipswich, (page 120) is one of the very best of all such signs, sporting as it does a steam engine with one container 'up back', plus another bogey (with container on top) in tow. The rig's glorious red, white and green livery is echoed in the overall design and lettering of the sign. This colour scheme occurs on the advertising of other removals firms, such as Samuel Hill (page 171). Estate agents' *'For Sale'* signs were formerly often made of enamelled iron (page 177), while several others can be seen illustrated in the reproduced catalogues.

Utilities

Until the 19th century, virtually all heating and lighting was provided by wood, charcoal, wax, tallow, organic oil and coal (page 175). Experiments with coal and methane gas street lighting had been attempted in the early 19th century, the technology for this leading eventually to the supply of domestic gas. The first electric street lighting, which was pioneered in London and Newcastle, was soon followed in the 1880s by the first domestic electric lighting, installed by Lord Armstrong at Cragside, his Northumberland estate mansion. The filament light bulb, having apparently been invented

simultaneously by Swan on Tyneside and Edison in the USA) (page 194), was soon in mass production, eventually superseding the domestic gas mantle (page 175). The new trade of electrical engineer was naturally advertised by the latest advertising medium, enamel signs (page 174). In most European cities, domestic heating as well as industrial power was provided by coal into the 20th century (page 175). Mr Therm, the mascot to the Gas Light and Coke Company, (page 175), precursor to British Gas, was designed by Eric Fraser in 1931.

Furniture

In the drawing office at Falkirk Iron, a far-off windowsill supports a small drawing of bedroom furniture (page 53). An actual sign based on this drawing can be seen high on a wall in one of the furnace kiln shops (page 52), but none has survived to be collected in recent times. It looks similar to an A & R Dean bedroom furniture advertisement, companion to the well-known A & R Dean brass bedstead sign (page 170).

Building materials, kitchen gadgets, paints

Suburban bliss meant the opportunity to furnish and decorate one's home in the styles and materials currently fashionable. While the less well-off tackled DIY even back in the 1890s, as in *Diary of a Nobody*, most household maintenance, repairs and decorating was bought in, as in the *Ragged Trousered Philanthropist*. The upsurge in DIY occurred in the late 1950s, promoted by the likes of the first television 'changing rooms' style guru, Barry Bucknell.

Though sanitary ware was much advertised in newspaper small ads, it seems that the only enamel to have survived is for an enamelled bath (page 171). Building materials, from bricks and mortar to roofing felt and window frames, frequently featured on enamel signs (page 173). Siddons saucepans (page 133) and some German and Belgian signs for enamelled hollow-ware are among the few promoting kitchen utensils to have survived. In Germany, in particular, 'range' style cookers and stoves (solid fuel, gas and electric) were advertised in enamel.

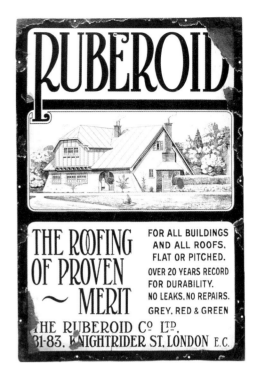

Telephone

Telephone handsets have never been advertised on enamels, because from their early days in the 1870s the phone companies rented them out. However, throughout the world, enamel signs have indicated the locations of public telephones. Examples from the USA, plus a few British, Irish and European are shown here.

Telephone lines

Phone companies the world over found that enamel signs were the most practical form of signage. The familiar bell icon symbolises a line installed by the Bell Telephone Co. Occasionally a telephone is pictured, usually of the 'candlestick' design. The only enamel sign that we have been able to locate which features a person using a telephone is this magnificent example, advertising margarine.

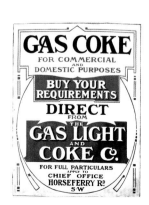

Financial institutions, Building societies, Banks & Insurance companies

Typical services included: Financial services.

The public was by far the biggest market that could be reached by street advertising, and was booming in size by the mid 19th-century, creating cities that were millions in number. With factory wages rising and greater discretionary spending power for more people than at any previous time, savings and investment business thrived. Owning the bricks and mortar that housed the family and its possessions was unusual for most families at that time. Most workers rented property from landlords, or received lodging as part payment in farm, pit, or factory cottages, with only a fortunate few retiring to charity cottages. Later in the century, skilled labourers in well-paid jobs aspired to own their own homes, but could not afford both rent and sufficient savings to make property buying feasible. Consequently the building clubs that had grown up in the 1770s to assist property purchase, evolved in the 1840s as permanent Building Societies. The Abbey National started in this way, as the National Permanent Mutual Benefit Building Society. Added to this title later were the words Freehold Land Society. Before universal suffrage, commoners were entitled to vote only if they owned freehold property to a certain value. Home owning therefore had two benefits, primarily to provide shelter, but also providing the freeholder with political power. Prudent householders also wanted to make sure, that all was not lost in the event of a catastrophe. Thus began the growth of dozens of insurance and assurance companies and societies. Not only could property and house contents be insured, but also other liabilities – life, health, businesses, travel, livestock and vehicles. Many enamel signs attest to the spread of the insurance market.

Those with enough money and property to not require the support of a building society had, since the late 17th century, kept their money in banks. A few of these institutions, like the Ulster Bank, (page 177), invested in dependable, long-lasting enamelled iron for their signboards. A typical feature of insurance and assurance companies was the use of elaborate coats of arms.

Agricultural, Horticultural requisites, Pet & other Animal Feed Suppliers & Veterinary

Typical stock/services included: Horticultural supplies, manure, seeds, animal husbandry products (feeds, liniment, sheep dip), farm machinery, agrochemicals agricultural tools, manure, guano fertiliser, cattle feed, patent animal medicines, lawn-mower sharpening services, seeds, gardening implements and gardening / country pursuits periodicals.

From the early 19th century an increasingly large population of economic migrant workers moved to the cities escaping virtual destitution as countryside employment disappeared. Traditionally, they had farmed their own small plots when not working for landowning farmers. It was natural for them to continue to augment subsistence factory wages by growing vegetables and keeping a pig in the back yard, until it was made illegal. If there was no cultivatable garden attached to the home, plots could be rented from the burgeoning allotment growers associations, which were well established throughout Britain by 1900. Seedsmen, like Webbs', supplied large specialist seed shops in every town and city. Colourful seed packets were installed on display racks in village hardware stores to cater to the needs of smaller communities. Webbs' narrow enamel signs would have flanked the doorways of hardware shops and seed merchants, or else have been placed on either side of shop windows.

Eventually, most defunct enamel signs were turned into scrap metal and junked. Often, thrifty gardeners obtained redundant signs for re-use as shanty walls, supports for compost heaps, leek trench dividers, anti-rabbit fencing and potting shed roofs. This secondary 'life' of street jewellery, in allotment gardens, was a happy chance that enabled plenty of specimens, to survive total destruction.

Household pets have been popular in Britain since animals were first domesticated in pre-historic times. Originally, dogs and cats were kept for their vermin control skills, but eventually specific breeds were developed for hunting or herding, or as companions to the young and the elderly. These pet varieties might be kept in the

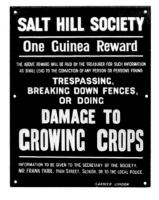

WEBBS'

Celebrated

SEEDS

Wordsley,
Stourbridge

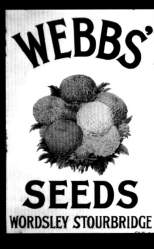

WEBBS'
SEEDS
WORDSLEY STOURBRIDGE

WEBBS'
SEEDS
WORDSLEY STOURBRIDGE

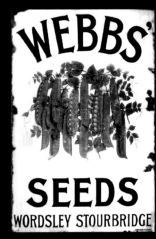

WEBBS'
SEEDS
WORDSLEY STOURBRIDGE

WEBBS'
SEEDS
WORDSLEY STOURBRIDGE

WEBBS'
SEEDS
WORDSLEY, STOURBRIDGE

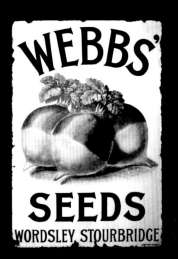

WEBBS'
SEEDS
WORDSLEY, STOURBRIDGE

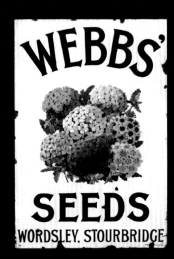

WEBBS'
SEEDS
WORDSLEY, STOURBRIDGE

WEBBS'

Celebrated

SEEDS

Wordsley
Stourbridge

home alongside songbirds such as linnets, larks and the like, housed in cages long before the now ubiquitous budgie arrived from the antipodes.

The movement of the greater part of the population to urban dwellings meant that previously commonplace wildlife food and offal by-products from home butchery were not available. Butcher's offal was in demand to feed poor humans; thus a trade in specialist pet foods began which still thrives today. Spillers made the first dog biscuits in 1855. As seems to be the case with most other products for which enamel advertising signs were made, a rash of minor manufacturers, represented now by a few scarce examples, such as Lowe's Carta Carna and Alpine blood salt, were ousted from the market by the most successful manufacturers. In the case of pet food the largest producers and the most prolific users of enamels, were Spiller's and Spratt's. Spratt's, Spiller's and Thorley's also widely advertised their products for farm animals using enamel signs. The Thorley's Ovum Poultry Spice, Spratt's Patent Chicken Meal and Elliman's Embrocation, are examples of advertising that cross the border between commercial and domestic markets. Spratt's pet food advertising campaign, using the letters of the product name modified to represent variously a Scottie dog, a cat, a budgerigar and a goldfish, counts among the cleverest, most economical uses ever devised of typography as a selling tool (page 183).

It may be of some significance that when street jewellery had all but disappeared from the streets of Britain, most surviving examples were to be found *in situ* on the walls of pet shops. In rural areas, the use of enamels to advertise products more suited to urban living was limited. However, a thriving industry in enamel signs advertising products useful to the farmer existed throughout Europe and the world at large. Numerous companies that manufactured sheep dips advertised by using enamel signs. Quite frequently, this type of sign had very large quantities of descriptive text, usually detailing awards to and the hammer price of prize specimens that had been successfully protected from infection (pages 181 and 216).

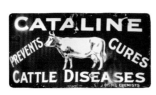

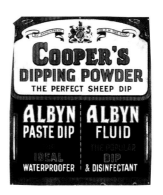

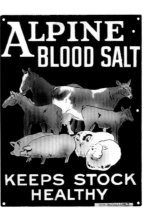

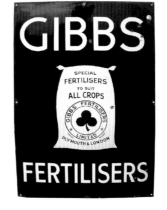

It's a dog's life

A mix of signs advertising confectionery, polish, washing products, pet food and flour encases this general dealer's corner shop in Crewe photographed c.1910. Note the three sizes of the Rowntree's 'Three generations' sign. A Melox advertising agent imitated the well-known Fry's sign, (pages 4, 5 and 131), in the anthropomorphic image on this postcard.

Digging for victory

Signs were sometimes 'rescued' from demolition sites and given new life as fencing in gardens and allotments. As long as the enamel was not chipped, the signs remained in good condition.

Music shop:

Typical stock/services included: Sheet music, musical instruments, records, gramophones and instrument hire.

The invention of the microphone and the phonograph in 1877 and radio in 1895, dealt a slow death to music performed in the home, terminating around 1920. From then onwards even humble homes could boast a wireless set and / or a gramophone. During the Victorian and Edwardian eras the parlour piano or harmonium reigned supreme as the focus of family life in the evenings and weekends, when singing popular songs or hymns was accompanied by the member of the family whose ability to 'tickle the ivories' was considered an accomplishment. Local dealers issued most enamel adverts for pianos. It was much rarer for piano manufacturers to issue signs, such as the Steinway, as in the Jordan's catalogue (page 66, (22)). Many working-class men, particularly mill and mine workers, joined brass bands. Boosey & Hawkes made a fortune selling brass instruments and sheet music, though enamels of these products are also rare. His Master's Voice and other recording companies issued enamels too, and the *trompe l'oeil* shiny groove of the record reproduced in enamel seems to have had special appeal.

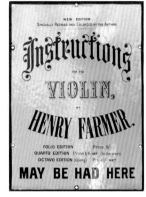

THE DRESDEN PIANO Co Ltd.

"The Dresden"
FOR PIANOS & ORGANS

BRANCHES & AGENCIES THROUGHOUT NEW ZEALAND

Columbia
RECORDS

Columbia
Grafonola

Columbia
Records

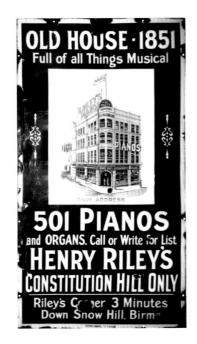

OLD HOUSE · 1851
Full of all Things Musical

501 PIANOS
and ORGANS. Call or Write for List
HENRY RILEY'S
CONSTITUTION HILL ONLY
Riley's Corner 3 Minutes
Down Snow Hill, Birm

"THE BRISTOL"
PIANO Co Ltd

"The Bristol"

FOR PIANOS
AND ORGANS

Branches & Agencies Everywhere

PATERSON & SONS
INSTRUMENTS ON HIRE

TUNING ORDERS RECEIVED

Columbia
Accredited Dealer

Spratt's

SINNER
Backpulver

DEPOT FOR
SILCOCK'S
POULTRY FOODS   CATTLE FOODS

Kodak

MÝDLO

ferrania

The medium is the message

Here are a few examples of how commercial artists have blended words and images.

ONOTO
THE PEN
FILLS ITSELF.
CANNOT LEAK.
CAN BE CARRIED AT ANY ANGLE
BRITISH MAKE

CHOCOLAT VILLARS

Cinema, Holiday resort seaside pier:

Typical stock/services included: Arcade machines, tea dances and sideshow entertainments.

Directional signs to Llandudno (page 185) and Yarmouth Pleasure Beach (below), an instruction plate from an amusement arcade fortune-telling machine and an on-site nameplate (New Palace Pier at St. Leonard's) though not strictly adverts, are enamel signs associated with holiday time. In the holiday spirit, the *Daily Sketch* sign *'There first'* (page 87), shows a seaside beach scene, and the Irish Sweepstake sign (page 185) savours a day at the races.

The signs advertising the Queen's Hotel and Grand Pleasure Tours (page 185) are both lavishly detailed with incident and information. A convertible limousine is pictured on the promenade before the Queen's Hotel. A coach and four, a twin-funnelled cruiser and an L&NWR engine with three Pullmans in tow, travel at speed across the centre of the Grand Pleasure Tours sign. The City of Durban official apartheid notice is a grim reminder that recreational fun has sometimes been a jealously guarded privilege. 'Sidney Bacon's Pictures' (below) is the only known cinema enamel sign.

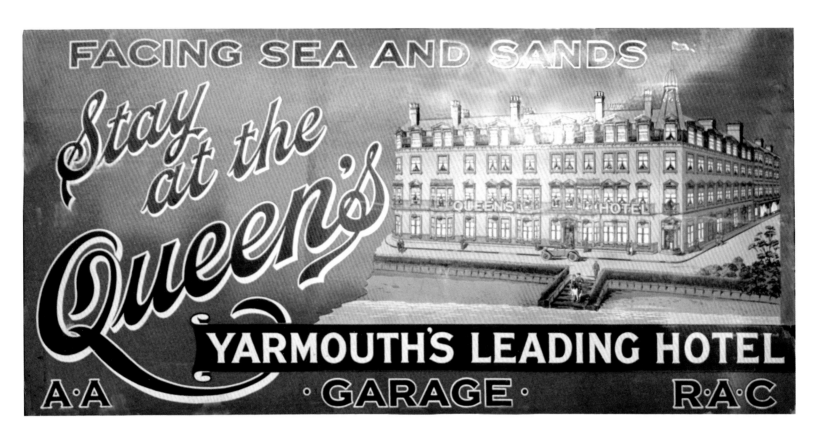

Typewriter supplier:

Typical stock/services included: Manual and electric typewriters, shorthand and business machines, dictaphones and typing requisites.

Shops specialising in the sale of typewriters and typing ancillaries disappeared around 1990 with the arrival of the PC and its superior word processing capability. The typewriter, once a potent icon of journalism and fiction writing, became a museum piece overnight. Invented in 1868, typewriters soon became an indispensable adjunct of commercial enterprise. Edison patented the first electric typewriter in 1872. The stock market and news bureaux used this as the ticker tape machine, which was not developed as an electric manual typewriter until the 1920s and was not a serious rival to purely manual typewriters until IBM developed a superior model in 1941. The typewriter was utilised in large office typing pools, where serried ranks of desks staffed by professional typists 'typed up' shorthand notes that had been dictated earlier.

Edison's phonographs (cylinder sound recording devices) were employed as dictaphones before being developed as commercial musical record players. The School of Shorthand & Typewriting sign, c.1900, (1) indicates the commercial importance of having these skills. The advantages of clarity and uniformity, plus the bonus of being able to instantly produce duplicate and triplicate copies, by inserting carbon paper between the typing papers, as in Pelikan Kohlenpapier (2), ensured good record keeping, accurate accounting and improved customer service. The press, military, educational establishments and private citizens who made their living by writing, took advantage of the new writing machines. The need for repair, spare parts, new models and typing supplies like ribbons, corrective papers and fluid, 'carbons' and typing paper, as in Pelikan Schreibbander (3), was catered for by local specialist shops, avoiding the delay and carriage costs of sending machines back to the original manufacturer.

Nipper types

The gramophone and gramophone record were the invention of Emile Berliner, a German-born US immigrant, who patented them in 1887. His success with manufacturing them in Europe from 1889, the founding of the Berliner Gramophone Company in 1895, followed by their promotion in Britain by William Barry Owen, later led to Owen and Trevor Williams setting up the Gramophone Company in London in 1897.

In 1897, photographer and painter Francis Barraud had the bright idea of painting, from a photograph, his brother's ratter, Nipper, listening to a phonograph recording and titled it 'His Master's Voice'. He submitted the painting to the Gramophone Company, who purchased it in 1900 for £100 and the perpetual copyright, provided the artist replaced the phonograph (an invention of Berliner's rival, Edison), with a gramophone. Also in 1900, the Gramophone Company bought the rights to the Lambert typewriter, renaming themselves the Gramophone and Typewriter Company. By 1911 His Master's Voice became their official trademark. The unique enamel plate above seems to be an abandoned attempt to create an advertising image that links the two products. Note that the engraving (on the wall) of the Nipper portrait is in reverse, and that the dog on the girl's knee is not the original Nipper, who died in 1895.

2

1

3

Jeweller, Watchmaker, Fancy goods retailer:

Typical stock included: Clocks and watches, jewellery, precious metal utensils and cutlery.

There is a plethora of enamel signs which advertise clocks, pocket and wrist watches. Omega, Ingersoll and Jaz are typical examples of firms whose advertising relied heavily on enamels. At a time when watches were very expensive because of their intricate mechanisms, and often gold casings, owners had them serviced regularly and repaired to extend their effective lives. Today, electronic watches are cheap enough to be discarded when fashion changes, and are indeed themselves becoming redundant as the mobile phone takes on the additional functions of timepiece, alarm, camera and sound recorder. As these innovations become standard, watch repair shops will disappear.

Few enamels signs were issued by the gem trade to advertise jewellery. Such rarity is one reason for including the horribly wrecked Geo. Dimmer sign (4). Its advertising copy mentions diamonds and pearls, watches, clocks, antiques, plate, jewellery and wedding presents, making this sign literally as well as metaphorically a true, if tarnished, example of street jewellery. Mr. Dimmer, like Rose & Bates (8) probably operated from a single premises, or like Saqui and Lawrence (5) from a couple of regional outlets beyond a London base, unlike H Samuel (7), whose chain of jewellers extended to many parts of Britain. Many jewellers boosted their incomes by selling giftware and ornaments, euphemistically known as 'fancy goods', such as Goss porcelain (6).

4

5

6   7

8

Government offices, Libraries, Post offices:

Typical stock/services included: Postal services, communications, licenses and policing.

Many main shopping streets were, and still are, punctuated by public buildings which house services requiring signage.

The usual type of letter box built into the walls of post offices was made by, and known as, a Ludlow. This is a wooden box clad in sheet steel panels, unlike the wall, lamp and 'pillar' box that is made in cast iron. Ludlows are easily distinguished from cast-iron wall boxes by having white enamel plates, sometimes with a posting aperture, and embellished with the Royal cipher of the monarch reigning when they were erected (1).

Recruiting to the armed forces and gaining employment through labour exchanges was, from the reign of Edward VII, a matter for public announcement via posters – famously *'Your Country Needs You'* – and occasionally through enamel signs (2). Within public buildings, enamel identification plates guided visitors to various offices located along the corridors of power, occasionally admonishing the public to be of good behaviour (4/5). While smoking in public places was allowed, spitting was prohibited as a TB risk (3 & 6). Similarly, official information, legal proscriptions and social directives were often conveyed to the public in sober black lettering against plain white backgrounds, on the unrelenting hard surface of enamel plates. Embassies and consulates generally display on the frontages of their buildings, an enamelled iron shield emblazoned with their country's national crest.

6

2

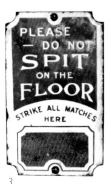
3

4

5

Photography shop:

Typical stock/services included: Cameras, film and paper, darkroom equipment, chemicals, processing and professional photography.

In the early days, during the half-century or so after its invention around 1839, photography was the hobby of intellectuals, scientists and the very wealthy, including many famous names such as Edward Muybridge, Lewis Carroll and Queen Victoria. Cameras were custom built by cabinetmakers; glass negatives, chemicals and papers were made at home.

Itinerant professional photographers like Matthew Brady sent teams with horse-drawn mobile darkrooms to cover news events like the American Civil War. The range of services needed to support the less well off amateur photographer did not emerge on the high street until the 20th century, encouraged by the success of the Kodak Box Brownie, launched in 1900. Commercially viable mass-produced cameras and photographic services soon followed throughout the world.

Examples of photographic imagery on early enamels signs are very rare. In addition, whereas pre-1900 opera glasses, binoculars and telescopes would be bought from an optician, from the early 20th century onwards, these commodities were to be had from a photography shop.

Bicycle shop, Gunsmith, Sports shop

Typical stock / services included: Bicycles & bike accessories, hunting, shooting and fishing gear, sports equipment and clothing, toys and games.

The popularity of angling, tennis, cycling and all cross-gender sports and hobbies, has never waned, although enthusiasm for some sports, such as toxophily and bowling, as in Carters lawn sign (page 191, 3), has lately been eclipsed by the likes of skateboarding and paragliding. Enthusiasm in Britain for target and rough shooting has been suffocated by draconian laws, but survives in the rest of the world. Enamel advertisements for shooting paraphernalia such as wet-proof coats and wellies, plus a dozen or so examples of signs advertising guns, gun sights and cartridges, attest to the sport's popularity. At one time, sports shops sold equipment for everything from snorkelling to cycling, though the latter has become so popular that many specialist cycling shops now flourish. Cycling produced some of the most elaborate and stylish poster art during the *belle époque* in France, and inspired a crop of enamels in Britain, rivalling in numbers and variants the many enamels for newspapers and tobacco products. Many spectacular European cycle enamels survive, such as Opel (1), NSU (2) and Maxwell (page 212).

2

"PHELAX"

RAIN RESISTING COAT

PROPERTY OF
ADIRONDACK LEAGUE CLUB
ALL PERSONS ARE FORBIDDEN TO
HUNT, FISH OR TRESPASS THEREON

ZEISS
ZIEL-FERNROHRE

Legia Star
HIGH SPEED
à
GRANDE PUISSANCE
POUR TOUS LES
TIRS à LONGUE DISTANCE
AUGMENTE DE 10 MÈTRES
LA PORTÉE DE VOTRE FUSIL
FABRIQUE NATIONALE D'ARMES DE GUERRE

SNOWFLAKE
CLEANS BUCK-SKIN & CANVAS BOOTS BEAUTIFULLY

COMMITTEE TEA TENT
PRIVATE.

(DEPOT FOR)
SLAZENGERS'
LAWN TENNIS
THE CHAMPIONSHIP
OF THE WORLD HAS BEEN WON
FOR 12 SUCCESSIVE YEARS WITH THIS RACKET.

BALLS FOR SALE
APPLY WITHIN

HURRICANE
MASQUES SOUS-MARINS

PLAYERS ARE REQUESTED
CAREFULLY TO
REPLACE THE TURF

TO THE
TENNIS TOURNAMENT

THE **"SUTTON MASTER"**
HARD TENNIS COURT
NO WATERING · NO ROLLING
· NO UPKEEP CHARGES
CONSTRUCTED BY
SUTTON & SONS, KINGS THE SEEDSMEN
READING.

ΤΑ ΚΥΝΗΓΕΤΙΚΑ ΟΠΛΑ ΠΙΠΕΡ
ΕΙΝΑΙ ΤΑ ΚΑΛΛΙΤΕΡΑ
ΖΗΤΕΙΤΕ ΤΟ ΑΝΩ ΣΗΜΑ ΤΟΥ ΕΡΓΟΣΤΑΣΙΟΥ

Anglers!
We sell and recommend
SPRATTS
SILVERCLOUD
GROUND BAIT
It keeps Fish in the Swim!

By Appointment · Seedsmen to H.M. The King

SOW YOUR LAWN
Carters
TESTED SEEDS

REMINGTON
WETPROOF

CURTISS & HARVEY'S
SMOKELESS
DIAMOND
CARTRIDGES
SOLD HERE

KYNOCH CARTRIDGES

B·S·A
RIFLES & GUNS
TRADE MARKS
B.S.A
WHOLESALE DEPOT

Der Deutsche Jäger
Jäger-Treffpunkt

JK
GUMMI-STØVLER
JK
HØJESTE KVALITET

KEEGAN
GUN MAKER

TUNET
LA CARTOUCHE DE QUALITE
EN VENTE ICI

Sewing machine shop:

Typical stock included: Sewing machines
and accessories and machine servicing.

Sew brilliant

The Singer sewing machine shop in St. Petersberg, c.1905 may be sporting on its frontage enamel signs similar to those issued for French, Spanish, Greek, Italian, Dutch and German-speaking countries, or they may be paper posters like the one reproduced (at right). Late Tsarist Russian commercial art was among the most elaborate, decorative and fanciful in the world. Happily a large archive of printed-paper examples has survived, though sadly no known enamel signs.

The Russian poster shows the seamstress wearing national costume. In most sewing machine enamel signs, changes in 'modern' dress fashion, between c.1900 and c.1950, can be observed, although Leticia seems a little underdressed.

When political incorrectness ruled

The Chatton furnishers sign, (page 170), as well as displaying some fashionable bamboo pieces, represents workers loading the van as comical figures. Many other signs, like Morse's Calcerium (page 173), and Fry's Burglars (page 213) convey a belittling impression of working people. Some other signs seem to be disrespectful in the representation of people of non-Caucasian race. Such illustrations reflect what by modern standards can be regarded as politically incorrect attitudes towards social class and race, endemic to both colonial politics and social attitudes of the time. However, illustrators were even handed in their mockery, as even the 'white' elite classes were satirised, as in the Passing Show 'Hush he's busy!' (page 99).

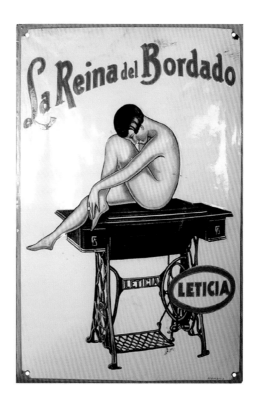

Electrical goods, Radio merchant:

Typical stock/services included: Electrical hardware, lighting fitments, personal electrical kit, radios and other audio equipment.

The 20th century electrical supplier was a specialist offshoot of the traditional hardware merchant from whom the earliest electrical fittings, such as light bulbs and socket plugs, would have been purchased. As more electrical gadgets such as toasters, kettles, radios, mangles and vacuum cleaners became readily available, the need for specialist outlets was created. Electrical shops often doubled as agents for electrical engineers, contractors and repairers. For a while this specialisation extended to shops devoted to selling and repairing radios and televisions. Even into the 21st century a few retail premises advertise themselves as 'shaver repair' shops.

The remarkable 1950s vintage four-piece Philips sign (1) pictures a wide range of electrical goods manufactured by Philips and sold at electrical shops.

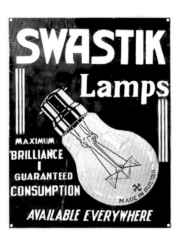

Charitable institution:

Frequent junking of the not very old is a relatively modern effect of disposable income. The urge to be charitable is not modern, but most secular charitable institutions have been set up with increasing frequency in the post-Tudor period, since when, the charity of religious foundations became less prominent. Until the mid 20th century most charities relied on cash donations deposited in collection boxes like that for the Shipwrecked Mariners Society (2).

Library:

Typical stock/services included: Books and periodicals and educational provision.

The library was once a mark of sophistication among the rich. Gradually, libraries became common public amenities, either through bequests made by philanthropist Andrew Carnegie, or by private lending associations, such as the Tabard library (4), or through the auspices of the local authority. When libraries required signage, it was often provided in enamelled iron. The 'Library Buildings' (3) sign is located opposite Willesden main library, close to the site of Garnier's factory, and may be the last enamel sign by that factory still in use in that locality.

Undertaker, Monumental mason:

Typical stock/services included: Funeral services and trappings.

Funerary traditions in many countries demand a portrait of the deceased on the grave marker. Miniature enamelled metal plaques have proved a popular vehicle for these. Signs for funeral parlours are the last word in advertising, often located at the dead centre of town.

Scrap merchant:

Typical stock/services included: Reclaimed metal.

The final resting place for most enamel signs was, alas, the scrap metal merchant's yard. Angus Gunn (5) probably gave the last rites to many hundreds of old enamel signs.

2

3

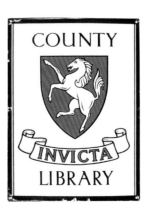

4

5

Transportation
Signs that oiled the wheels of progress

Without the canal, road and rail transport innovations of the late 18th and early 19th centuries, the speed and impetus of the industrial revolution could not have been achieved; indeed the process would have stalled. Until these improvements to travel and haulage were in place, journeys of any sort, including commercial deliveries, were accomplished on foot or by horse, on mainly un-metalled roads, or by river and coastal sea routes. Transport network development became, through necessity, the concern of powerful, wealthy individuals or local civic organisations (such as Turnpike Trusts) in pursuit of profit. The Third Duke of Bridgewater had a canal built by James Brindley to facilitate the transport of coal from his mines in Worsely to Manchester, where it could be sold profitably. Construction was given the go-ahead in 1759 and the canal opened in 1763. It was effectively, if not technically, the first commercial navigational canal in England, inspiring through its success numerous others, until a countrywide network was established. It soon became apparent that goods of all types (including fragile items like Wedgwood ceramics) could be safely transported by canal, with much less damage and delay.

Improvements to road quality soon followed in 1765, from when until 1792 'Blind' Jack Metcalf was engineer to Britain's first modern quality cambered, drained roads. Thomas Telford, having followed Metcalf's example, surpassed his achievements with the Shrewsbury to Holyhead Road, which included his masterpiece, the Menai suspension bridge. The third of the great trinity of British road engineers was John MacAdam, whose granite chip amalgam became the most economical and thus, from c.1815, the most widely used road surface.

Wooden wagonways, used in mining operations from at least as early as the 1550s, were developed as iron railroads, first for transporting goods at the Surrey Iron Railway in 1803, then for passengers in1807 when the Mumbles Railway opened, both using horse-drawn carriages. These ancestors to the modern railway were challenged and superseded by the steam locomotive railway, originated in 1804 by Richard Trevithick. His innovation was 'forgotten' until George Stephenson's

Railway trains were rarely depicted on enamel signs, but major stations like Paddington (right), suburban platforms and trackside buildings, offered perfect support for the signs. Enamel was easily cleaned, resistant to chemical corrosion and impervious to weather effects. Paper posters were suitable for short life advertising purposes, but enamels held their own as semi-permanent advertisements capable of withstanding the atmospheric assaults of the dirtiest railway shed. Enamel signs would shine up as good as new; street jewellery sparkled in any location, whether on the street or in a station.

World travellers
The LEP sign is a unique example of an enamel depicting three major modes of modern freight transport, air, rail and sea. Vorwarts adds into the equation four types of cart, plus a sledge, forms of goods carriage traditional for millennia before the modern automated machines represented in the LEP sign. Oxen, mules and horses represented in the four signs here, were some of the main draught animals used to haul wagons or to bear riders.

Shanks's pony

Stepping out together, a constable and parlour maid are putting their best feet forward to advertise in the Wellington Journal & Shrewsbury News *(4). Getting there on two legs, carrying goods in a back pack like this Swiss mountaineer, (5) or just going for a stroll like the beau in Guinea Gold (2), was until the introduction of mass-produced bicycles, the normal means of personal transport available to those who could not afford a horse. (Note the shadow of the bobby on the beat in pursuit of the cheeky crossing sweeper). Samuel Butler's photograph of Fleet Street in May 1899 (1) shows London pedestrians surrounded by adverts. The Fry's advertising postcard (3) makes the point well by showing a foot-slogging Scotsman being refreshed en route from John 'o' Groats to Land's End with a cup (embellished with the name Fry's) of cocoa. Note also the Fry's enamel sign above the café window and other Fry's adverts on distant buildings.*

1

2

3

4

5

In the frame

Usually, enamel signs were supplied with no frames, being screwed, nailed or stapled to walls using pre-drilled screw holes or else just the edges for support. Some enamels have no screw holes, indicating that these were supplied with wooden frames. Occasionally, frames were 'built in' pictorially, as is the case with Grant's Stand Fast Whisky *(page 113) and the* Perth Dye Works *(5). The greatest number of signs surviving with frames intact are Ogden's, such as the St. Julien (1), which additionally has screw holes. Guinness published signs with cast brass frames, complete with integral screw lugs (4) and some in wooden frames (3). Pullars of Perth issued a sign (2) with a Gothic style, carved and gilded wooden frame, which they later imitated in die-cut enamel, (5) which was cheaper to produce!*

1

4

2

5

3

redeveloped steam locomotives, which first operated at the Stockton to Darlington railway from 1825.

Sailing ships have provided long distance transport for passengers and goods from ancient times, famously by the far travelled Phoenician traders. With improvements in hull and rigging technology during the 1840s and 1850s came the introduction of 'clipper' ships, whose speed enabled rapid conveyance of tea and other goods to and from geographically distant locations. Between 1783 and 1812 experiments in France, the USA and Britain led to the successful use of steam-driven propulsion for ships. This was perfected in 1838 when Isambard Kingdom Brunel's *Great Western* won the first trans-Atlantic steam-powered race. When in 1845 Brunel's *Great Eastern* set the standard in propulsion by screw propeller, the age of the ocean going steamship began in earnest.

Horseback or carriage transport remained the norm for local journeys until the invention of the bicycle. Around 1790, Comte Mede de Sivrac of France invented the earliest bicycle, called a *celerifère*. Kirkpatrick MacMillan, a Scottish blacksmith, devised a bicycle with foot pedals in the 1830s, but it was not until the French carriage makers, father-and-son team Pierre and Ernest Michaux invented an improved bicycle in the 1860s, that the machine gained general acceptance. Chains with sprockets were added in the 1880s, as were air-filled tyres.

The concept of an internal combustion engine was first described in the Renaissance, by da Vinci and during the late 17th century by Christiaan Huygens. Experiments in the 19th century by many individuals, including Lenoir, Carnot, Otto, Daimler and Maybach, concluded with its successful application, as a stationary engine, in 1879, by Karl Benz. In 1885 Benz applied his new technology to make the world's first automobile. The internal combustion engine was later adapted to power trains, boats and planes. Powered flight was first successfully pioneered by the Wright brothers (USA) in 1903. Rapid innovation and growth in the late 18th century, helped fuel the industrial and social revolutions which, having started in Europe in the late 18th century, spread worldwide within a hundred years.

In this chapter we present enamel signs decorated with imagery and text that reflect contemporary attitudes to and celebrate these transport revolutions.

Canals

When the Patent Enamel Company's founder, Benjamin Baugh, had a factory built at Selly Oak, Birmingham in 1889, solely for the production of enamelled iron advertising signs, he ensured that the plant was served by dedicated canal and rail branches, as well as being situated near existing road systems. Canal transport was still a vital element in guaranteeing the delivery and dispatch of raw materials and manufactured goods. The raw materials for making signs – wrought iron, frit, clay and oxides – were bulky, heavy items of the kind that horse-drawn canal craft had been reliably delivering for over a century. Rail transport, though operating via an already massively developed rail network, was relatively expensive, but had the advantage of speedy delivery; horse-drawn drays were still vital for local deliveries. Benz's invention of the motorcar was still only four years old; it would be twenty years before the pre-eminence of horses would be threatened by delivery vehicles powered by internal combustion engines. Indications of road, rail and canal networks can be observed on the Falkirk Iron Company complex, Webb's Seed factory and Mitchell & Butler brewery aerial views (page 49). The only known enamel sign bearing a pictorial rendering of a working canal, advertises a grate polish called Nixey's Silver Moonlight; surely a most extreme case of product promotion by an inappropriately romantic brand name. The romanticisation is obtusely compounded by a lush visual association with *La Serenissima*. The delicacy of violet and yellow tones in the rendering of the Venetian night sky reflected in the Grand Canal is, it must be conceded, among the more subtle achieved in this relatively coarse medium.

Roads

Roads *per se* are so rarely shown on enamel signs, that the Durant sales / service depot advert (page 137) seems to have no subject at all. The road is represented as a white curve, vanishing towards a sunset horizon. However, the lure of the 'open road' is well conveyed by this visual device. Until 1885 horsepower on the roads meant just that; the whole road system was supplied with all the necessities of supporting and supplying horses. Everything for their

animals, from stables to hitching posts, from watering troughs to crossing sweepers, was available to riders, coachmen and drovers. The road surface over which the car in the British Dominions Service Agent sign is speeding (page 199) throws up small macadam stone chips, showing that this remote Highland highway had not yet been coated with tar.

Railways

Enamel signs were conceived and first issued contemporaneously with the boom period of railway engineering. Many engravings and photographs attest to the symbiotic relationship between the two. The railway environment proved to be very friendly to enamel signs and other, more ephemeral poster advertising. Indeed advertisers continue to target railway passengers at mainline and underground stations. The identification plates, called totems, that used to adorn railway station platform pillars and lamp-posts were enamelled plates coloured appropriately in the livery of each railway company. London Underground totems went through a whole series of forms including various geometric shapes, until the design settled as a circle crossed horizontally by an oblong text box. Many other informational signs on railways were created as enamelled iron plates. Images of trains on enamel signs are uncommon. Those that survive include several removals and storage company adverts and the magnificent Indian *British Express Butter* (page 147) and the Chinese safety warning sign (page 201). The best of all rail travel signs which includes a train, steam cruiser and stagecoach, advertises the Caledonian Railway (page 185).

Enamel signs affixed to slot machines situated at railway stations, were regularly and widely used as instruction plates, price labels and adverts. Examples illustrated on page 202 include vending machines for dried dates (5) and chewing gum (2), a platform ticket vending machine (4), a waiting room sign in an elaborate cast iron bracket and sign, presumably once affixed to a machine used for vending railway timetable guide booklets (3).

Carriages, taxis, buses, motor coaches

The most celebrated enamel sign image of a carriage is the Cadbury's landau (page 128). A rare glimpse of a speeding stagecoach is afforded in the right-hand oval cartouche of the Caledonian Railway *Grand Pleasure Tours* sign, (page 185). Not a single image of a rickshaw, sedan chair, palanquin or palkee can be found in enamel, but one image of an early motorised taxi, and a list of officially approved fares for Hackney carriages survive. The one shown (page 205) is dated 1st June 1872, and while this date probably relates to the relevant byelaw, it is likely to be contemporaneous, and suggests that this may be one of the earliest dateable enamel signs. The badges worn by taxi, tram and bus drivers, and the local authority licensing plates displayed on Hackney carriages were usually also white enamel with black text (page 205).

Trucks / Lorries / Cars / Motorbikes

Signs bearing images of traction engines, the immediate precursors to the petrol / diesel powered lorry, appear elsewhere in this book. Bernard, a French marque of lorry, uses this neo-classical figure to emphasise the strength combined with grace of their wagons. The MAN and VOMAG signs (page 207) make lorries look almost as glamorous and powerful as the ocean liners pictured later.

Images of cars abound in many advertising contexts, from being incidental details in views of department stores and hotels to more auto-specific appearances, like advertising headlamp bulbs and petrol. However, signs advertising specific cars are not very common, *Mein Benz* (page 207) being a splendid exception to the rule! There are several enamel signs of the badges or crests for different makes of motor car.

The macho drama of biking is exemplified in the Schüttoff and NSU Motorräder signs. Leathers, goggles and militaristic uniforms and symbolism abound in these advertisements. We have yet to find enamels promoting biking accessories such as helmets or goggles, but occasionally, as in the Hutchinson tyres sign, motorcycle tyres are specified.

Small craft and sailboats

As a symbol of old-fashioned gallantry, adventure and historic 'soundness', the sailing ship has few rivals in advertising imagery. Among the examples shown here, sailing ships and boats advertise products as diverse as coffee, motor oil, insurance, chocolate and motorcars.

Ships and liners

One of the all-time great advertising images is the 1935 poster *Normandie* by Cassandre, in which the great liner is viewed bow-on as from a tugboat (unfortunately never produced as an enamel sign). It was a thrill on first finding a cache of Holtzapfel's *Mauritania* enamels, to realise that this similarly dramatic image must pre-date the *Normandie* by a decade or so. On pages 208-209 can be seen many other carefully composed Art Deco poster-inspired enamels featuring ocean liners, plus some less brilliant depictions of great ships, including Gdynia-Amerika Linien which look as if they have sailed off a naval architect's drawing board. Included in this section are two advertisements for trunks, an essential piece of luggage for those voyaging on steamers. The association of things naval with rum and tobacco is well known, so a couple of enamels featuring sailors (advertising Unsere Marine cigarettes of 1916 and, of a similar vintage, a sign for Peter's Old Navy Rum) have been included with the other sea-faring signs.

Aeroplanes

Collectors eagerly seek the precious few enamel signs depicting aeroplanes. The USA seems to have produced most enamels relating to this subject, particularly promoting fuels for aircraft, but few of these (apart from the three illustrated, Socony, Smith-o-Lene and Harbor) are actually illustrated with planes. The ENSA *Munitions Concerts* enamel is especially rare in that it depicts a WWII bomber, plus the smoking barrel of a huge field or navy gun, and two rows of heavy ammunition. Few other pictorial enamels directly produced as a result of either World War survive, apart from a few depicting military insignia. At one time it was a common sight to see a single engine biplane soaring over urban areas, leaving vapour trails that spelled out advertisements – usually for events like circuses – and occasionally the names of products. The product name is being 'sky written' by just such a bi-plane in the background of the Rim Orange Juice sign.

The hazards of transport These four signs illustrate graphically some of the hazards of transport use.

Above: A panoramic view of Harrow on the Hill railway station, produced from six separate photographs taken in 1933. Many slot machines on station platforms had enamelled plates fixed to them. The Fry's Cocoa advertising postcard has Fry's written on the cup, and shows a Fry's enamel sign staked out by the track (page 203).

This explanation of the meanings of the letter puzzles on Hudson's soap adverts not only satisfies our curiosity about those cryptic acronyms. It also implies, by the heading 'A Railway Puzzle Explained', that the main arena for siting these particular signs was on railway properties. Note however, that other sites such as shop fronts were also used, as in the Gateshead shop (page 7).

2

3

4

5

This picture of North Walsham station c1902 is from a large archive of photographs taken around that date. Evidence from these photos and written documentary evidence, has enabled members of the M & GN Circle to establish the distribution of adverts at the time. The preponderance of Pears soap 'blister' signs indicates a campaign in progress. The signs would have been removed en masse, once the campaign had run its course.

The view of Pelaw station platform, plus several anonymous station corridors and sidings with enamel signs in situ, show the wide distribution of enamel signs throughout the public areas of stations.

Alfred Cathie at Lewisham Junction (right) and Fleet Street, (page 198), were taken in the 1890s by novelist Samuel Butler and are reproduced by permission of the Master and Fellows of St. John's College, Cambridge.

Platform puns

The Sunday Pictorial enamel visually puns with the coach-painted inscription of a First Class railway carriage. The Daily Mirror claims that it is 'best all along the line', again suggesting that it is First Class by using two giant figure '1s' with only tiny 'Ds' (for one penny).

Tinplate and enamel toys

Two tinplate railway station models with accurate reproductions of enamel signs. A Stower's Lime Juice Cordial is depicted on the right of the tinplate model railway waiting room. A paper poster of the same advert is on the hoarding illustrated (page 126). The miniature Bassett-Lowke tinplate adverts for Bovril, Capstan, Oxo and Gold Flake are shown with a Euro for scale. The tinplate Chocolat Menier colonne Maurice is decorated with French enamel signs. Many companies issued miniature enamelled brass brooches, in imitation of their 'grown-up' street jewellery enamel adverts. The most famous of these, were the many series of Robertson's 'gollies' of which the Jolly Golly golfer was the original, issued in 1928.

2

4

1

Horse-drawn vehicles and motorbuses were used routinely as mobile advertising platforms. Adverts covered much of the exterior and interior surfaces, including the staircases, for which specially designed signs were made (1/3/5). Iron Jelloids (5) would have been fixed to a stair riser, while Heinz and Plummers (1/3) were cut and trimmed to curve round the staircase. Dey Time Registers (page 186) is curiously 'out of true' to facilitate easy reading when placed on a staircase.

Bus driver Percy Burdge, standing between an inspector and a conductor beside their 48 Paddington Green bus, at Abbey Wood Plumstead Garage in 1920, is wearing an enamel licence badge. Cab licence plates (4) were also manufactured in enamelled iron.

This photograph gives us a rare glimpse of a classic sign, the Wincarnis lady, in situ, in the company of two less exotic, but equally rare Beasley's Ales & Stout signs.

3

5

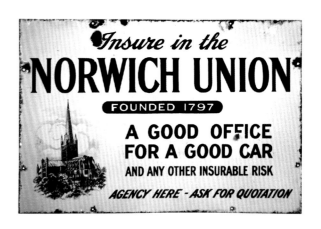

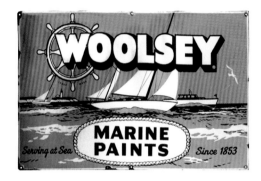

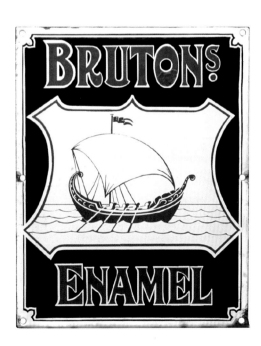

CUNARD LINE
VERTRETUNG HIER
U·S·A & CANADA

HOLLAND WEST·AFRIKA LIJN
AMSTERDAM

HOLLAND WEST AFRICA LINE
CORRESPONDING SERVICES TO AMSTERDAM VIA

CUNARD LINE
COMFORT.
FOR CELERITY.
CIVILITY.

GDYNIA-AMERIKA LINIENs
EKSPRESRUTER
KØBENHAVN - HALIFAX - NEW YORK
8 DAGE
KØBENHAVN - GDYNIA - 15 TIMER
REGELMÆSSIGE AFSEJLINGER
TIL BRASILIEN - URUGUAY - ARGENTINA

VIKING MELK

CUNARD LINIEN
Expresruter til
Amerika og Canada
Verdens STØRSTE og
HURTIGSTE Dampere
Aut. Agent:
VILH. BREDO
Aarup

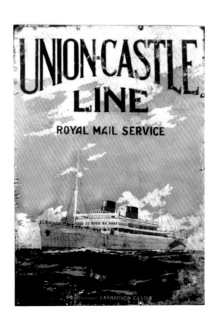

UNION CASTLE
LINE
ROYAL MAIL SERVICE

AGENTUR
Holland-Amerika Linie

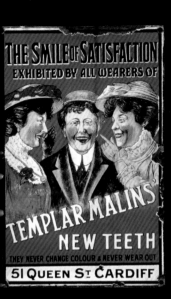

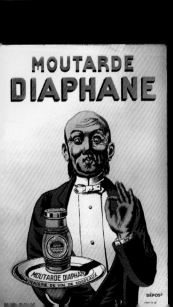

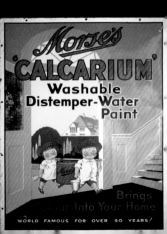

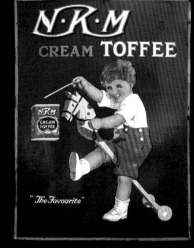

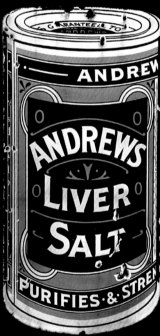

MURAD
THE TURKISH CIGARETTE
Everywhere—Why?

MAYO'S PLUG
LIGHT AND DARK
SMOKING
COCK O' THE WALK

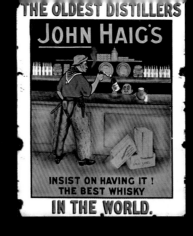

THE OLDEST DISTILLERS
JOHN HAIG'S
INSIST ON HAVING IT!
THE BEST WHISKY
IN THE WORLD.

und Bären Eier Maccaroni

SEIFENFLOCKEN
LUX
SUNLICHT GES. A.G. MANNHEIM

H.P. HOOD & SONS
MILK

Clean your Carpets at home
Largest sale in the world
CHIVERS' CARPET SOAP
SIMPLE & SURE
SOLD EVERYWHERE

ETABLISSEMENTS
A. LECOMTE
A.L

CONDENSED MILK
MILKMAID BRAND
ANGLO-SWISS CONDENSED MILK CO.
CHAM, Switzerland, and LONDON.

Korsør Løve
Vegetabil Margarine

ANIS DEL MONO
VICENTE BOSCH BADALONA ESPAÑA

Dr. E.L. GRAVES
UNEQUALED
TOOTH POWDER
FOR HEALTH AND BEAUTIFUL
TEETH

LITTLE'S SHEEP DIPS
Fluid   Powder
BRIGHT STRONG WELL GROOM FLEECES WITH BEAUTIFUL LUSTRE AND SOUND TIP
FREE FROM ALL INSECT LIFE
THESE DIPS ARE UNEQUALLED FOR QUALITY QUANTITY AND PRICE
MORRIS, LITTLE & SON LTD
DONCASTER, ENG. BROOKLYN, N.YORK, MELBOURNE VIC PORT ELIZABETH AFRICA AND CHRISTCHURCH, NEW ZEALAND.
THE UNIVERSAL VERDICT WHERE   LITTLE'S DIPS ARE USED

HOFHERR·SCHRANTZ·CLAYTON·SHUTTLEWORTH·BUDAPE

HSCS

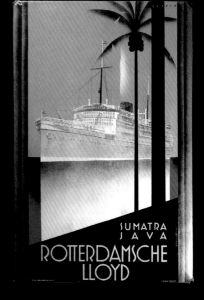

SUMATRA
JAVA
ROTTERDAMSCHE
LLOYD

KÖNIGLICH
HOLLÄNDISCHER
LLOYD
AMSTERDAM

NACH SÜD
AMERIKA

LIPTON'S

TEA
MERCHANTS

BY SPECIAL
APPOINTMENT

"CARBO-GONFLEUR"
SPARKLETS
BREVETÉ S.G.D.G.
EN VENTE ICI

Reckitt's
BLUE.

PIERCE
FARM MACHINES & IMPLEMENTS

PIERCE VICTOR
MOWERS

SOUND VALUE IS THE PIERCE
GUARANTEE OF SATISFACTION

ASSOCIATED
MOTORWAYS

ROUTE MAP
REGULAR DAILY SERVICES

BOOKING OFFICE

VERTRETUNG DER
HAMBURG-AMERIKA
LINIE
UNITED AMERICAN LINES

ELECTRIC

JUPITER

Products & inventions timeline

1807: *Gas street lighting: Pall Mall, London, UK*

1814: *Jerimiah Colman starts mustard business: UK*

1832: *Dr Henry Stephens invents writing fluid: UK / Winsor & Newton artists' colourists founded: UK*

1835: *First large-scale outdoor poster: Jared Bell, New York USA*

1837: *William Proctor and James Gamble establish their soap and candle business: USA*

1840: *Isaac Reckitt establishes Reckitt & Son: UK / Justus Liebig develops concentrated meat extract: UK*

1845: *Birth of Co-op movement in the UK*

1846: *Free Trade established in the UK / Last horse-drawn mail coach in the UK*

1848: *Yale pin-tumbling cylinder lock: USA / Pre-Raphaelite Brotherhood founded: UK / WH Smith open railway bookstalls: UK / Omega watchmakers founded: Sweden*

1850: *Isaac Merritt Singer invents sewing machine: USA / 'Clipper' sailing ships bring cheap tea from Far East / Porcelain enamelling on iron: UK & USA / Reckitt's starch handbills and posters: UK / Exterior advertising first used on street railways: USA*

1851: *Great Exhibition: London, UK with first 'spend a penny' public lavatories / First manufactured soap in bar form by Bratt: USA*

1852: *Henri Giffard invents powered airship: France / First safety matches: UK / V&A museum opens: UK / William Cooper develops sheep dip: UK / Reckitt's Blue in production: UK / Aquascutum tailoring brand & shop chain founded: UK / First British post box: Guernsey*

1853: *Elisha Otis invents safety lift: USA / George Crum invents potato crisps: USA / Cadbury's awarded Royal Warrant: UK / Gossage patents cleanser formula: UK / Gevalia coffee: Sweden*

1854: *Colman's employ 200 in Norwich works: UK*

1855: *Bessemer steel converter: UK / Lundstrom safety match: Sweden / Repeal of newspaper tax laws: UK / Spiller's dog biscuits: UK / Standard letter box with enamelled plates on sides and aperture in London: UK*

1856: *William Perkin supplies world's first synthetic dye: UK*

1857: *Baugh's Bradford Street. factory: Birmingham, UK / Gallagher's cigarettes founded: Ireland / Standard wall mail boxes introduced: UK*

1858: *Isambard Kingdon Brunel's 'Great Eastern' launched: UK / Pasteurisation invented by Louis Pasteur: France / Internal combustion engine: Lenoir, Belgium*

1859: *Baugh takes out patents on enamelling leading to Patent Enamel Company: UK / Public drinking fountains introduced: UK / Proctor & Gamble sales exceed one million dollars*

1860: *Cigarettes in Europe / Birth of Alphonse Mucha: Czechoslovakia / Ogdens founded: UK / First Vélocipède: Michaux, France / Morris & Co. founded: UK / Fry's centenary: UK / Spratt's dog biscuits marketed: UK / 20 ad agencies in NY, USA*

1862: *Guinness registers trade mark: Ireland / Rowntree's founded: UK*

1863: *Sir Henry Bessemer perfects steel production: UK / Cast iron coal hole covers introduced: UK*

1864: *Birth of Toulouse-Lautrec: France / Victory 'V' sweets factory opens: UK / Robertson's marmalade introduced: UK*

1865: *Louis Pasteur invents Pasteurisation: France / Lloyd's bank centenary: UK / Galleria shopping arcade opened: Mangoni, Milan, Italy*

1866: *Birth of Dudley Hardy: UK / Cadbury's produce cocoa essence: Birmingham, UK / John Penfold designs hexagonal pillar box: UK*

1867: *Alfred Nobel invents dynamite: Denmark / World Exhibition: Paris, France*

1868: *First traffic lights installed: London, UK Christopher Sholes invents typewriter: USA / Birth of Will Bradley, Art Nouveau artist: USA / Birth of John Hassall: UK / Patent Enamel Co. enamelled plates fixed to Liverpool mailboxes, thereafter used nationally: UK*

1869: *Margarine introduced: France / Brooke-Bond Tea Co. founded: UK / J Sainsbury founded: UK / Anderson & Campbell formed, forerunner of Campbell's Soup Co: USA*

1870: *John Wesley Hyatt invents celluloid: USA / Abolition of soap tax: UK*

1872: *Thomas Edison invents ticker tape machine: USA / Birth of Edward Johnston (typographer for London Underground): UK / Birth of Aubrey Beardsley: UK*

1873: James Eno patents Eno's Fruit Salt: UK / First Co-op goods manufactured: UK / Horlicks founded: USA

1874: Birth of Winston Churchill: UK / Quaduplex telegraph invented: Edison, USA / First Impressionist exhibition: Paris, France / Horlicks launched in UK / Abbey Building Society founded: UK / The Post Office adopts red for letter boxes: UK

1875: Arts & Crafts Movement, c.1875-c.1900 / Hudson's soap factory opened, Liverpool, UK

1876: Alexander Graham Bell patents telephone: USA / Heinz founded: USA

1877: Thomas Edison invents phonograph: USA / Introduction of the microphone: Cuttris, USA & Siemens, Germany / John Player founded: UK

1878: Birth of Frank Pick, key man to the development of London Underground / Quaker Oats launched as first mass-marketed breakfast food: USA

1879: Werner von Siemens builds first electric tram: Germany / Joseph Swan's filament lamp: UK / Cadbury's Bournville factory opens / First electric street lighting: London, UK

1880: Socialist Workers formed, France / Vending machines for postcards introduced in UK / James Bonsak patents cigarette rolling machine: USA / Refrigerated meat shipped from Australia to UK / Norman Shaw designs Bedford Park Garden Suburb, London: UK

1881: Electric lighting in Houses of Parliament, London: UK / Hotzapfel's compositions registered in UK / Slazenger sports company founded: UK

1882: Henry Seeley invents electric safety iron: USA / Hugh McKay invents combine harvester: Australia / Bird's custard first pictorial adverts: UK / Chesterfield, the first city to be wholly lit by electric street lighting: UK

1883: Daimler develops petrol engine: Germany / Benz & Daimler factories open: Germany / Lewis Waterman patents pen inventions: USA

1884: Fabian Society formed: UK / James Ritty cash register: USA / Ankastrum enamel works: Sweden / Gaudi's Sagrada Familia church in Barcelona: Spain

1885: Eastman photographic dry plates & film: USA / Benz motor car: Germany / Lever introduces Sunlight soap; advertisements erected in north of England railway stations: UK / Carreras launch Black Cat cigarettes: UK

1886: Aluminium invented by Hall, USA & Herault, France / Bartholdi's Statue of Liberty opens in New York: USA / Coca Cola launched: USA / Heinz issue enamel signs: UK / Hovis founded: UK

1887: Hannibal Goodwin invents celluloid film: USA / Tolbert Lanston patents hot metal type: USA / Olofstrom open enamel factory: Sweden / Eiffel Tower opens in Paris, France

1888: Dunlop pneumatic tyre: UK / Emil Berliner's, shellac disc record: USA / EW Fyffe established: UK / Raleigh establish Nottingham bicycle factory: UK / WD & HO Wills launch Woodbine cigarettes: UK

1889: Josephine Garis Cochran invents dishwasher: USA / Kodak introduces roll film: USA / Jules Chéret awarded la légion d'honneur: France / Benjamin Baugh builds Selly Oak factory: UK / 'Buck' Buchanan establishes American Tobacco Co: USA / Carroll's Mick McQuaid tobacco brand: Ireland / John L Johnston forms Bovril Company /UK

1890: Art Nouveau, c.1890-c.1914 / Birth of Stanley Morrison, designer of Times New Roman: UK / Reckitt's launch Zebra grate polish and 'Bag Blue': UK / Hovis established, UK

1891: Thomas Edison patents kinetograph: USA / Jesse Reno invents escalator: USA / Paul Gauguin goes to Tahiti / Birth of Aleksandr Rodchenko, constructivist painter and photographer: Russia

1892: Anarchist demonstrations Paris, France / John Froelich invents tractor: USA / Eros statue by Sir Alfred Gilbert, unveiled in Picadilly, London: UK / WH Smith centenary: UK

1893: World Fair: Chicago, USA / The Studio magazine first published: UK / Player's register Hero trademark: UK / Schultze & Wehrman open enamel factory: Germany / William Wrigley Jr introduces Juicy Fruit and Spearmint chewing gum: USA

1894: *Lumière brothers invent cinematograph: France / Aubrey Beardsley's Salomé published: UK / Robert Dold enamel factory opened: Germany / John Harvey Kellogg invents cereal flakes: USA*

1895: *Marconi invents radio: Italy / Gillette safety razor introduced: USA / HG Wells' The Time Machine published: UK / Schweppes centenary: UK Gottfried Dichanz opens enamel factory: Germany / Wilhelm Röntgen invents x-ray imaging: Germany*

1896: *Death of William Morris: UK / Wincarnis on sale: UK / Guglielmo Marconi sends his first radio signal: Italy*

1897: *Cathode ray tube: Braun, Germany & Thompson, UK / Otto Leroy, enamel factory opens: Germany / Reckitt's launch Robin starch: UK / Shell registered in London, UK / Street monuments (clocks, etc.) erected to celebrate Victoria's Diamond Jubilee / Michael and Eugene Werner build first motor cycle: France / Felix Hoffman synthesized aspirin: Germany / Campbell's Condensed Soup invented: USA / Pearl B Wait invents Jell-o: USA*

1898: *Valdemar Poulsen invents magnetic recording: Denmark / Garnier, enamel factory opened: London, UK / Pepsi Cola invented by Caleb Bradham: USA*

1899: *Monkey Brand soap launched: UK / Tobler chocolate launched: Switzerland / First stamp vending machine introduced: UK / Liebig's Extract marketed as Oxo: UK*

1900: *Ferdinand, Graf von Zeppelin's first air ship flight: Germany / British Labour Party founded: UK / Eastman Box Brownie camera introduced: USA / HMV logo 'Nipper' registered: UK / Ever-Ready, batteries marketed in UK / Leibig's Oxo liquid sold in UK / Non-standard telephone boxes: UK / Milton Hershey's chocolate bars go into production: USA*

1901: *Death of Queen Victoria / H Cecil Booth invents vacuum cleaner: UK / Bryant & May launch Swan Vesta matches: UK / Satori Kato 'invents' instant coffee: USA*

1902: *Willis Carrier invents the air conditioner: USA / George Claude invents neon light: France / James Mackenzie invents lie detector or polygraph machine: UK / Oldsmobile is the first US car to be mass produced / Pepsi Cola comes to the market: USA / Marmite invented: UK*

1903: *Michael Owens' first automatic bottle making machine: USA / Wright brothers first manned, powered flight: USA / Marks & Spencer founded: UK / Ty-Phoo Tea launched: UK / Cherry Blossom boot polish launched: UK / Ira Washington Rubel invents offset printing: USA / Mary Anderson patents the car windscreen wiper: USA / Ford Motor Company formed: USA / Willem Einthoven invents the electrocardiogram (ECG): Netherlands / Albert J Parkhouse invents the wire coat hanger: USA*

1904: *Sigmund Freud publishes Psychopathology of Everyday Life: Austria / Thomas Sullivan invents teabags: USA / Ovaltine launched: Switzerland / Canada Dry launched: UK / Dr Pepper soft drink launched nationally: USA / Grace Weidersheim creates hugely popular 'Campbell's Kids' to market Campbell's products: USA / Thomas Sullivan introduces tea bags to a world market: USA*

1905: *Einstein publishes General Theory of Relativity: Germany / Cadbury's Dairy milk chocolate launched: UK / Packard car factory opens, Detroit: USA / First use of reinforced concrete: USA / First Yellow Pages published: USA / US Congress passes Pure Food & Drug Act / Brasso metal polish introduced: UK*

1906: *Arsonval and Bordas invent freeze drying: France / First mass-produced electric washing machine: USA / 'Everyman' library founded: UK / Cadbury's launch Bournville cocoa: UK / Kiwi shoe polish launched: Australia / William Kellogg invents Cornflakes: USA / US Congress passes Meat Inspection Act / The Poor brothers registered the Osram light company: USA / Kellogg's Cornflakes enters the market: USA / Glaxo is registered as a trademark for dried milk: UK*

1907: Royal Dutch/Shell Group formed: UK & Netherlands / Lumière brothers invent colour photography (autochrome lumière): France / Birth of Cubism, c.1907-c.1917 / Peter Behrens creates the world's first corporate image for AEG: Germany / Leo Baekeland invents bakelite: USA

1908: Lever buys Hudson's soap (retaining name): UK / Jacques Brandenberger invents Cellophane: Switzerland / First Model T Ford on sale for $850: USA / JW Geiger and W Müller invent the geiger counter: Germany / Fritz Haber invents the Haber process for making artificial nitrates: Germany / General Motors formed under Billy Durant: USA / Oxo sponsors London Olympics: UK

1909: Kraft Bros. incorporated (Kraft Foods): USA / Chlorine first added to public drinking water: USA / Thomas Lipton begins blending tea in New York: USA / Quaker Puffed Wheat, invented by Alex Anderson, comes to the market: USA / Charles Wakefield produces Castrol lubricant: UK

1910: Oxo cubes launched UK / (Hudson's) launches Rinso: UK / Morris Motor Co. launched in Oxford: UK / Thomas Edison demonstrates the first talking motion picture: USA / Georges Claude displays the first neon lamp in Paris: France / The Oxo cube launched: UK

1911: Airmail post introduced: UK / Charles Kettering invents self-starting car ignition: USA / Mazola, the first refined corn oil, is marketed: USA

1912: Kiwi shoe polish marketed in UK / Clarence Crane creates Life Savers candy: USA / First tank patented by Lance de la Mole: Australia / Richard Hellman, a New York deli owner, markets Hellman's mayonnaise: USA

1913: Harry Brearley invents stainless steel: UK / Mary Phelps Jacob creates the brassiere: USA / Stravinsky, Russia: Rite of Spring / Armory Show, NY, USA / Ford automobiles in mass production: USA / Georges Claude displays neon advert for Cinzano: in Paris: France / Arthur Wynne invents the crossword puzzle: UK / Parcel Post delivery begins: USA

1914: Outbreak of WWI / First £1 and 10/- notes issued, UK / Vorticist magazine Blast: UK / Fry's Turkish Delight introduced: UK / Wrigley's Doublemint introduced: USA

1915: Sullivan and Taylor invent Pyrex: USA / Cadbury's Milk Tray introduced: UK / Lipton's Tea incorporated: USA

1916: Birth of Dadaism at Cabaret Voltaire, Zurich, Switzerland / Clarence Saunders opens the first self-service store Piggly Wiggly: USA / Margaret Sanger opens first birth control clinic: USA / Kellogg's All-Bran introduced: USA

1917: Russian Revolution / Nekal - the first range of detergents: Germany / The Jazz Age c.1917 – c.1939 / Wood & Schraap, enamel factory opened: Netherlands

1918: WWI Armistice / Charles Jung invents Fortune Cookies: USA

1919: Hitler forms Nazi party / Mussolini forms Fascists / Alcock & Brown fly the Atlantic / Bauhaus founded by Walter Gropius: Germany / Carroll's Sweet Afton cigarettes introduced: Ireland

1920: Prohibition in USA means coffee sales boom / Art Deco style c.1920 - c.1940 / Earle Dickson invents 'Band-Aid': USA / Cadbury's Flake introduced: UK

1921: Famine in Russia / Thompson sub machine gun invented: UK / Huntley & Palmer's merge with Peak Frean to form Associated Biscuits: UK

1922: Ralph Samuelson invents water skis: USA / Herman Standinger develops polymers: Germany

1923: Austin 7 launched: UK / First neon advert installed for Packard: USA / Clarence Birdseye 'invents' frozen food: USA

1924: First Labour government, UK / Harwood develops self-winding watch: UK / British Empire Exhibition: UK / Gilbert Scott designs K2 telephone kiosk: UK

1925: Bell invents electrical sound recording: USA / Koekelburg opens enamel factory: Belgium / Betty Oxo created: USA

1926: General Strike: UK / John Logie Baird demonstrates the first television: UK / Erik Rothheim invents aerosol can: Norway / Proctor & Gamble introduce Camay soap: USA / ICI formed from four largest chemical companies in the UK / Beechams Powders introduced: UK

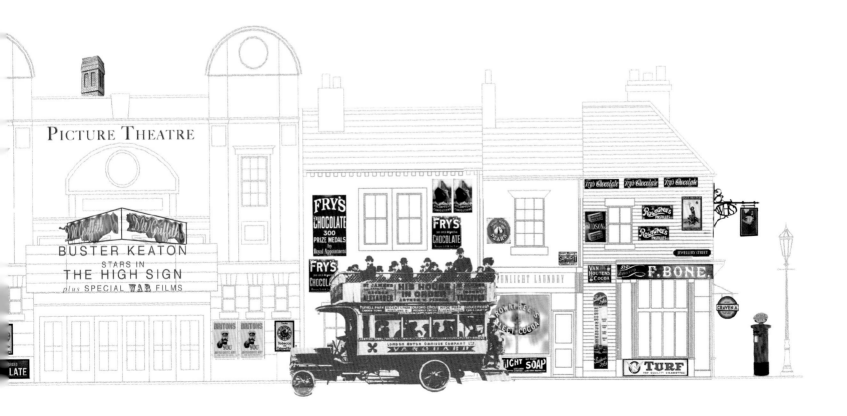

1927: Socialist riots, Vienna, Austria / First 'talkies': USA / Eric Gill creates 'Gill Sans' typeface: UK / Birth of Ed Benguiat, type designer: USA / Reckitt's market Karpol car polish / l'Emaillerie Alsacienne enamel factory opened: France / Automatic bread slicer/wrapper invented by Otto Rohwedder: USA / Erik Rothheim patents aerosol spray can: Norway

1928: Paul Renner creates 'Futura' typeface: Germany / Alexander Fleming discovers penicillin: UK / Birth of Adrian Frutiger, type designer: Switzerland

1929: Wall Street crash: USA / Trotsky expelled from Russia / George Eastman shows the first Technicolor movie: USA / Enzo Ferrari launches car company: Italy / Fyffe's Blue Label branding launched: USA

1930: Amy Johnson solo flight to Australia / Two million telephones & three million radio licences in the UK / Michael J Cullen opens first supermarket: USA / Shreve, Lamb & Harman design Empire State Building New York: USA / Ruth Wakefield launches the chocolate chip cookie: USA / Proctor & Gamble buys Thomas Hedley, soap mannufacturers, to gain foothold in UK market: USA

1931: Ford Motor Co. plant in Dagenham opens: UK / First Bedford trucks hit the road: UK

1932: Gillette launches Blue Gillette blade / USA / Grote Reber and Karl Jansky invent radio telescope: USA / Death of Jules Chéret: France / Aldous Huxley writes Brave New World: UK / ICI launch Perspex / Carl C Magee invents the parking meter, first used in Oklahoma City in 1935: USA

1933: Reg Gibson and Eric Fawcett discover Polythene: UK / Charles Darrow invents Monopoly: USA / Berthold Lubetkin forms modernist Tecton architectural practice: UK / Dettol goes on the market: UK / Proctor & Gamble launches Dreft washing powder: USA

1934: Arthur H Compton invents fluorescent light bulb: USA / Percy Shaw patented cat's-eyes for road safety: UK / Focke-Wulf the first helicopter: Germany / Proctor & Gamble launches Drene shampoo: USA

1935: Robert Watson-Watt invents radar: UK / Wallace Caruthers invents nylon: USA / 30mph speed limit introduced: UK / Penguin paperbacks appear: 1936 / Kreuger Brewing Co. first to use the beer can: USA

1936: Surrealist exhibition, London / Boulder Dam completed USA / Mignon typewriter company changes name to Olympia: Germany

1937: Frank Whittle's jet engine tested: UK / Walt Disney's Snow White, first feature length cartoon: USA / Nestlé invents instant coffee using a freeze-drying process: Switzerland / Northern Foods formed: UK

1938: Chester Carlson files for electron photography (photocopy) patent: USA / Laszlo Biró invents ball point pen: Hungary / Reckitt & Sons and JJ Colman merge to form Reckitt & Colman / Cadbury's Roses chocolate launched: UK

1939: World's Fair, New York: USA / British Overseas Airways Corp. (BOAC) formed: UK / Hewlett Packard founded: USA / Nylons first sold in USA

1940: Fall of France / Battle of Britain / London Blitz / Lascaux caves discovered: France

1941: Wartime 'Utility' style UK, c.1940-c.1950 / Igor Sikorsky flies first modern helicopter: USA / Penicillin mass produced: USA

1942: Oxfam founded / Enrico Fermi builds first nuclear reactor: USA / Edward Hopper paints 'Nighthawks': USA / Kodak launch Kodacolor, the first colour negative film for prints: USA

1943: Jacques Cousteau invents aqualung: France / Turing, UK: 'Colossus' computer / Tide washing powder launched by Proctor & Gamble: USA

1944: Walpamur produce 90,000 gallons of white paint for striped aircraft for D-Day landings: UK / Willem Kolff invents kidney dialysis machine: USA

1945: Vitamin A synthesised / Fashion magazine 'Elle' founded: USA

1946: Atom bomb tested on Bikini Atoll / Louis Réard creates the bikini: France / UNESCO established / Percy Lebaron Spencer invents microwave oven: USA / Birds-Eye launches frozen peas: UK / Tide washing powder launched in UK / Peter Goldmark demonstrates Colour TV: USA

1947: Indian Independence / Edwin Land invents Polaroid camera, on sale in 1948: USA / Tennessee Williams publishes 'A Streetcar Named Desire': USA / Dr Jonas Salk discovers polio vaccine: USA

1948: State of Israel founded / Apartheid commences in South Africa / Columbia Records launch first LP: USA / George de Mestral invents Velcro: Switzerland / Morris Oxford launched: UK / Alfred Mosher Butts invents Scrabble: USA / One million homes in USA have colour TV

1949: People's Republic of China founded under Mao Tse Tung / Arthur Miller publishes 'Death of a Salesman': USA / Ford Prefect launched: UK / Municipal gas companies vested into twelve area gas boards: UK

1950: China invades Tibet / 'McCarthyism' coined to describe anti-communist movement in USA / Diners Club and American Express introduce credit cards: USA

1951: Festival of Britain, London, UK / Carl Djerassi invents contraceptive pill: USA / Kodak launch first low-price Brownie movie camera: USA

1952: Hydrogen bomb invented / Eisenhower elected President: USA / Samuel Beckett publishes 'Waiting For Godot': Ireland

1953: Death of Joseph Stalin: Russia / Elizabeth II succeeds George VI: UK / Hugh Heffner launches 'Playboy' magazine: USA / Olympia typewriter model SG1 launched: Germany

1954: Sunsilk shampoo launched: USA / Fuller, Pearson and Chapin invent first solar battery: USA / Kodak launch Tri-X, high speed monochrome film: USA

1955: Birds-Eye fish fingers launched in UK / Crest toothpaste launched in UK

1956: Ford Zodiac launched: UK / Brooke Bond PG Tips' 'chimps' make advertising debut: UK / Kodak launch Verichrome Pan film: USA

1957: Schweppes Bitter Lemon launched: UK

1958: Glaxo acquires Allen & Hanburys: UK

1959: Barbie Doll launched by Mattel Inc: USA / Unilever launches Flora, the first margarine in a tub: UK

1960: Spratt's acquired by Spillers and receive a new set of brand identities:

2000: Garnier having been abserbed by Burnham were subsequently taken over by Stocksegus.

Bibliography
Monographs on enamel advertising signs

Street Jewellery Christopher Baglee & Andrew Morley, New Cavendish Books, London, England 1978

Blechplakate Alex Riepenhausen, F Coppenrath, Germany 1979

Emaille Borden J Stalkenborg & J van Zadelhoff, Uiteverij de Viergang, Netherlands 1979

Geëmailleerde Reklameplakkaten (catalogue) (revised) Verleden & Tijd-Schrift, VKM, Ghent, Belgium 1979

Svenska Skylatar B Conradson & O Nessle, LTS, Stockholm 1980

Emaile Plakate U Feuerhorst & H Steinle, Harenburg, Germany 1981

More Street Jewellery Christopher Baglee & Andrew Morley, New Cavendish Books, London 1982

Les plaques emaillees publicitaires (catalogue) Michel Wlassikoff, Galerie PEP, Paris, France 1983

Le plaques emaillees Michel Wlassikoff, Galerie PEP, Paris, France 1983

Les joyaux des rues Frederic Ghozland, Jadis, France 1984

Email Reklame Schilder Andreas Maurer, Zurich, Switzerland 1986

Email-Reklame-Schilder 1900-1960 Andreas Maurer & Klaus Pressman, Waser Verlag, Zurich, Switzerland 1986

Email Plakate Sylke Wunderlich, Edition Leipzig, Germany 1991

Cherchez la Femme Galerie Comes, Vienna, Austria 1991

Encyclopaedia of Porcelain Enamel Advertising Michael Bruner, Schiffer, USA 1994

Email & pub 1894-1994 P Courault & F Bertin, Pollina SA, Locon, France 1994

Le plaques emaillees Michel Wlassikoff, Editions Alternatives, France 1995

Emailschilder (catalogue) Erhard & Evamaria Ciolina, Battenberg, Augsburg, Germany 1996

Emailschilder und Reklame Susanne & Alexandre Zacke, Heyne, Germany 1996

More Porcelain Enamel Advertising Michael Bruner, Schiffer, USA 1997

Das Grose Buch der Emailplakate Sylke Wunderlich, Orbis Verlag, Germany 1997

2000 plaques emaillees & toles diverses (catalogue thematique) Jurgen Renke, Documenta, Belgium 1998

Email & pub 1894-1994. 100 ans de plaques emaillees Francais (revised) P Courault & F Bertin, Editions Ouest-France, Rennes, France 1998

Nothing Too Large! Nothing Too Small! The Story of Garnier & Co. Ltd (revised) Vera Thompson, Vera Thompson, London 1998

Enamel Advertising Signs Christopher Baglee & Andrew Morley, Shire Publications, Princes Risborough, England 2001

La folie des plaques emaillees Magdeleine Ducamp, Flammarion, Paris, France 2002

La plaque emaillees belge Mario Baeck & Jan de Plus, Weyrich Edition, Belgium 2002

Gadens Blikfang John Juhler Hansen, Forlaget Jelling, Jelling, Denmark 2002

Enamel Advertising Signs (new edition) Christopher Baglee & Andrew Morley, Shire Publications, Princes Risborough, England 2005

Street jewellery on show

Beamish, North of England Open Air Museum Beamish, Co. Durham DH9 0RG. T: 0191 370 4000. www.beamish.org.uk

Black Country Living Museum Tipton Road, Dudley, West Midlands DY1 4SQ. T: 0121 557 9643. www.bclm.co.uk

Blists Hill Victorian Town Madeley, Telford, Shropshire TF7 5DU. T: 01952 583003. www.ironbridge.org.uk

Bluebell Railway Sheffield Park Station, Uckfield, East Sussex TN22 3QL. T: 01825 720800. www.bluebell-railway.co.uk

Brewhouse Yard Museum Castle Boulevard, Nottingham NG7 1FB. T: 0115 915 3600. www.nottinghamcity.gov.uk/sitemap/brewhouse_yard

Brookside Miniature Ranway Macclesheld Road, Poynton Cheshire SK12 IBY. T: 01625 872919. www.brookside-miniature-railways.co.uk

Cadbury World Cadbury Limited, Bournville Lane, Bournville, Birmingham B30 2LU. T: 0121 451 4159. www.cadburyworld.co.uk

Flambards Village Theme Park Helston, Cornwall TR13 0QA. T: 01326 573404 www.flambards.co.uk

How We Lived Then. Museum of Shops & Social History, 20 Cornfield Terrace, Eastbourne, E Sussex BN21 4NS. T: 01323 737143.
   www.sussexmuseums.co.uk/how_we_lived_then.htm

London's Transport Museum Covent Garden London WC2E 7BB. T: 020 7379 6344. www.ltmuseum.co.uk

Milestones-Hampshire's Living History Museum West Ham Leisure Park, Churchill Way West, Basingstoke, Hants RG21 6YR. T: 01256 477766.
   www.milestones-museum.com

Montacute TV Radio & Toy Museum 1 South Street, Montacute, Somerset TA15 6XD. T: 01935 823024. www.somerset.gov.uk/somerset

Motoring Memories, Colyford Filling Station, Swanhill Road, Colyford, Devon EX24 6QQ. T: 01297 553815

National Cycle Collection The Automobile Palace, Temple Street, Llandrindod Wells, Powys LD1 5DL. T: 01597 825531.
   www.cyclemuseum.org.uk

National Motor Museum John Montagu Building, Beaulieu, Brockenhurst, Hampshire SO42 7ZN. 01590 612345. www.beaulieu.co.uk

National Museum of Gardening Trevarno Estate Gardens, Crown Town, near Helston, Cornwall TR13 0RU. 01326 574274. www.trevarno.co.uk

National Railway Museum Leeman Road, York YO26 4XJ. T: 01904 621261. www.nrm.org.uk

National Waterways Museum Llanthony Waterhouse, Gloucester Docks, Gloucester GL1 2EH. T: 01452 318200. www.nwm.org.uk

Severn Valley Railway The Railway Station, Bewdley, Worcestershire DY12 1BG. T: 01299 403816. www.svr.co.uk

Shambles Museum Church Street, Newent, Gloucestershire GL18 1PP. T: 01531 822144. www.shamblesnewent.co.uk/main.htm

The Stephens Collection Avenue House, East End Road, Finchley, London N3 3QE. T: 020 8346 7812. www.london-northwest.com/sites/stephens

Ulster Folk & Transport Museum 153 Bangor Road, Cultra, Holywood, Co. Down, N Ireland BT18 0EU. T: 028 90 428428.
   www.nidex.com/uftm

York Castle Museum Eye of York, YO1 9RY. T: 01904 687687. www.yorkcastlemuseum.org

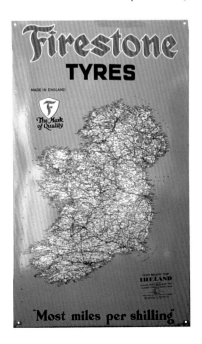

Index

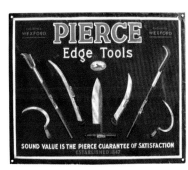

Picture index

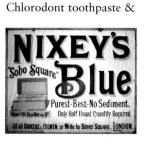

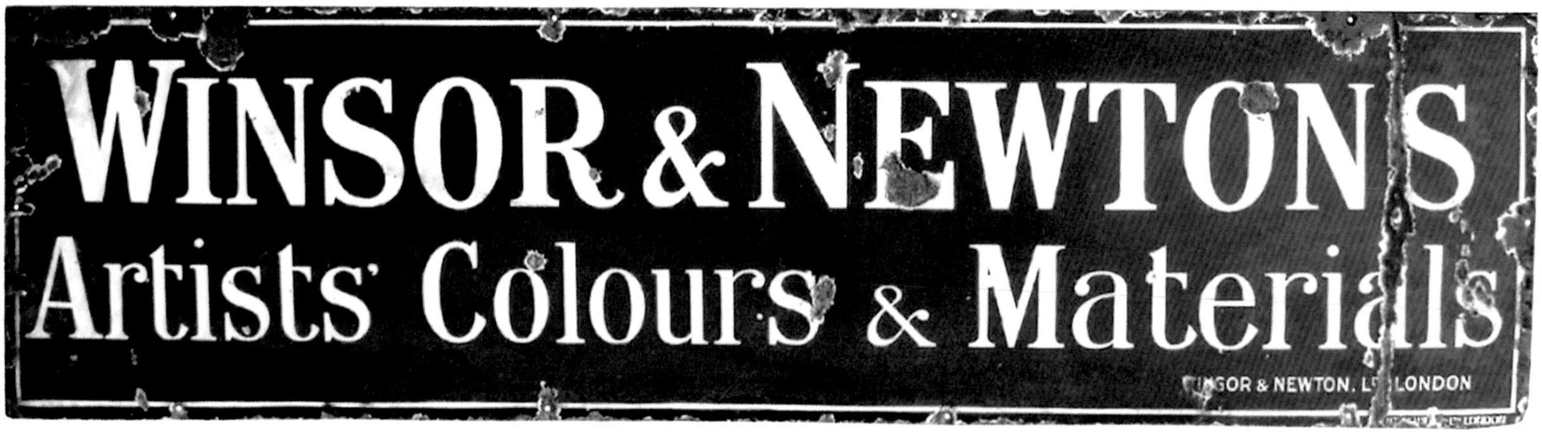
WINSOR & NEWTONS
Artists' Colours & Materials

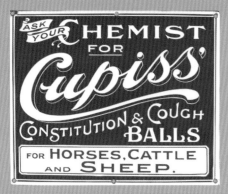

ASK YOUR CHEMIST FOR **Cupiss'** CONSTITUTION & COUGH BALLS FOR HORSES, CATTLE AND SHEEP.

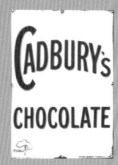

CADBURY's CHOCOLATE

AGENCY LAW UNION & CROWN FOUNDED 1825 A.D. Insurance FIRE. Company

Agent for P. & R. HAY. Established Over 100 Years Dyers & French Cleaners Edinburgh.

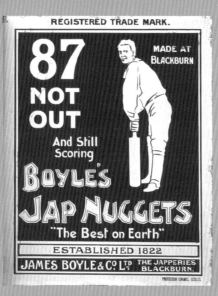

REGISTERED TRADE MARK. 87 NOT OUT And Still Scoring MADE AT BLACKBURN BOYLE'S JAP NUGGETS "The Best on Earth" ESTABLISHED 1822 JAMES BOYLE & Cº Lᵀᴰ THE JAPPERIES BLACKBURN.

Packard Service

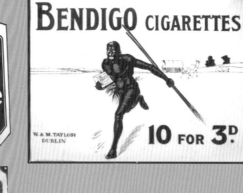

BENDIGO CIGARETTES W. & M. TAYLOR DUBLIN 10 FOR 3ᴰ.

DUNVILLE'S V R WHISKY

CONDENSED MILK MILKMAID BRAND Swiss CONDENSED MILK CHAM. Switzerland and London

TAYLOR & Cºˢ STAINES ESTBᴰ 1849. HIGH TABLE CLASS WATERS SODA LITHIA SELTZER POTASS LEMONADE ETC ETC TO BE OBTAINED AT ALL LEADING GROCERS. TRADE MARK

WILL'S's CELEBRATED GOLD FLAKE CIGARETTES 10 for 6ᵈ 20 for 1/-

KING COLE TEA YOU'LL LIKE THE FLAVOR

BORWICK'S BAKING POWDER The Best for every Home

Pascall's Confectionery

2,000,000. TWO-MILLION PEOPLE DRINK BROOKE, BONDS' TEA EVERY DAY. SOLD HERE, & BY AGENTS EVERYWHERE.

ASK FOR PILLS MADE BY PARKINSON'S

MACNIVEN & CAMERON'S PENS WAVERLEY PICKWICK PHAETON OWL PEN SOLD EVERYWHERE ARE RECOMMENDED BY 3050 NEWSPAPERS

THE "NUGGET" POLISH AS USED IN THE ROYAL HOUSEHOLDS

DON'T FORGET YOUR OXO cubes AND FRAY BENTOS SOUPS

CHOCOLATE CREAM